Boer War Diaries of Geldenhuys

Cover design by © Prop Geldenhuys Peysoft Publishing
Contact: oupey@editek.co.nz

Other books by the author:

- Rhodesian Air Force Operations
- Rhodesian Air Force Operations with Air Strike Log
- Nickel Cross – biography
- Operation Miracle – A Tribute to three bold Airmen
- Rhodesian War Casualties
- Rhodesian Memorials
- Geldenhuys Genealogy – 12 Generations
- Rhodesia - Zimbabwe Roll of Honour: 1965 - 1980

First published as ISBN: 978-1-920315-467
Just Done Productions Publishing 2009

This e-pub and revised edition published 2014
Epub ISBN: 978-1-31256115-1
ISBN: 978-0-9941154-2-3

Paeroa
2014

The Anglo-Boer War Diaries Of Jan Geldenhuys

Translated by his Grandson
Preller Geldenhuys

Book cover designed by John Dovey

Contents

Jan A. and A.C.F.Preller GELDENHUYS
05 September 1931

Jan with son Preller Geldenhuys, the author's grandfather and father

Foreword

My interest in the Anglo-Boer War 1899-1902 stems from reading my grandmothers account and then discovering that my grandfather's diaries were lodged with the Bloemfontein Museum. This resulted in publishing "*The Anglo-Boer War Diaries of Jan Geldenhuys*" in 2009. The Boer and Briton dispute in South Africa is known by several names: the War of Independence (*Vryheidsoorlog*), the Second War of Independence, the Great Boer War, the South African War and the Engelse Oorlog. The second Anglo-Boer War occurred over another British attempt to annex the Transvaal. This time the Boers were defeated.

My grandfather, Johannes 'Jan' Albertus Geldenhuys was affectionately known as "Oudad". He fought against the British who were assisted by the New Zealanders, Australians, Canadians, Indians and other colonial forces. Oudad was very active in the initial Western Front battles and later in the Transvaal and Free State - from October 1899 to April 1902.

Oudad Jan was born in July 1877 on Doornspruit Farm in the Kroonstad district of the Orange Free State; and died in May 1944 and is buried on his Rustpan farm, Bothaville.

My sister Delene and I visited the war museum in Bloemfontein on 15th May 2007 and were handed a typed copy of our grandfathers 'war memoirs' (*Oorlogsherinneringe*). His personal diary was completed as a banished (*banneling*) prisoner of war in Umballa, India. He documented his war experiences till Thursday, 20thNovember 1902.

The visit to the Bloemfontein museum was my second, in as many years, and proved just as emotional to me, personally, as my first visit. I wept. Unashamedly! My very good lady, Rina understood my feelings and was very supportive that I should write this story. Not my story, but 'his-tory' as documented by my grandfather over one hundred years ago.

It was a real privilege, and a source of great satisfaction, that I had my sister Delene and her husband, Stu McColl, from New Zealand, to go through the Museum. We carried out a tour of the Western Campaign Battlefields Route to Kimberley and Paardeberg. Stu's camera came in very handy to photograph statues and things of interest as they appear in this book.

The war diary started on 3rd October 1899 and covered the initial siege of Kimberley, the Battles of Belmont, Graspan/Enslin, Twee Riviere (Modder River) and notably Magersfontein. A short period of 'Hands Up' followed, then taking up arms again, "veg en vlug" (fight and flight), farm burnings, concentration camps, death of their first-born, capture, banishment to India, life and death in British prisoner of war camps. It ends rather suddenly, arrival back at Kroonstad, re-uniting with my grandmother and new-born son on the 20th November 1902.

The boere (Boers) tended to refer to themselves as 'burgers', translated as citizens, and thus named the war the Burger Oorlog literally translated Citizens War. New Zealanders tend to refer to the conflict as the South African War.

The stark differences in fighting philosophy cannot better be expressed than from a Boer's own lips: "You English fight to die: we Boers fight to live". Ponder that prophetic statement for a while – it explains much of 'Veg en Vlug' – Fight and Flight tactic so successfully embodied in guerrilla warfare strategy: so successfully developed and honed by none other than that great Orange Free State Vegcht Generaal – Fighting General Christiaan de Wet.

The translation of the 'high Dutch / Holland" language as spoken and written at that time was quite a challenge. The diary was written well before Afrikaans itself developed. The clarity of speech amazed me – and I can appreciate the good education that my grandfather must have had in the late 1800's. I don't think they were too concerned with, or knew much about paragraphing. Even in accounts that I got from my father-in-law (Francois Daniel Malan), he often wrote without full-stops. One had to re-read bits here and there to establish where one sentence ended and where the next started! However, what is indeed noteworthy is the chronology of events over a period of three years, written in pencil, and ended up with over sixty pages of typed script. No wonder my grandfather was always appointed adjutant / scribe or secretary to the numerous Boer officers' that he served. He also was a teacher to the children that were interned at Umballa POW camp in India.

Children!? Indeed! In fact, of the 40 prisoner of war camps world-wide, the Hinson Island camp specifically interned young boys to prevent them joining their elder brothers, cousins, uncles or fathers from taking up arms.

This e-pub edition came about after reviewing the book I published 5 years ago but now includes some New Zealanders I learned while living on the Coromandel peninsula.

Preller ("Prop") Geldenhuys
Paeroa
November 2014

War Memories (Oorlogsherinneringe)

The Year 1899

Anna Elizabeth Preller, 1879 - 1976, was the writers grandmother. She published her recollection of the Anglo Boer War in 1954 and I have merged her account with that of my grandfather, Johannes Albertus Geldenhuys.

She was better known as Lizzie Geldenhuys while my grandfather was called Oudad Jan.

Boer wedding

Her wedding was described by Dot Serfontein's *Amper Onse Mense.*

"Abraham Christoffel Naudé Preller was delighted that cold winter's morning on 27th June 1899, when his daughter Lizzie – one of the most beautiful ladies from the Onder-Vals – married Jannie Geldenhuys.

Around the white-washed stone-church of the small town Bothaville the esteemed of the North-West Free State stood. The men were dressed in neat tailored suits, with heavy watch-chains in the embroidered waistcoat pockets; the beards are lopped, the hair curls smeared with springbuck fat and pressed into shape with scented water. The women are standing in groups, with their umbrellas on their shoulders, shielding them from the cold southerly wind. Their watered jaconet velvety gowns, gathered and full of tucks and pleats, the unmistaken camphor smells of distinction.

Mother and baby photographed in the Kroonstad Concentration Camp

Jan Steyn, the owner of Lace Mine, a diamond mine near Bothaville, with his striped dress-coat, light brown trousers and white gloves, is in control of the reins. When he entered through the church gate the thin wheels of the black, landau cut grooves in the lose sand, spluttering the stone poles with stones.

How lovely Lizzie Preller looked in her white mervilleux wedding gown, on the arm of her father as the wedding march was played on the peddle-organ, as she approached the groom – beautiful in the sense of well-formed, but also beautiful because at that moment the inheritance of a proud ancestors was visible in her young face; the grey eyes of the Preller's, prominent high forehead and nose-bridge which rises high above the eyes, the slim, bony and nervous traits of the Dreyers, the blossom complexion of the Naudé's and the fiery manner of the Botha's.

Dot Serfontein (the writer) got to know Lizzie when she was already in her nineties, and from this bodily beauty the crux still discernible – still the bright eyes, the pride, and the vigilant spirit. She was then a truly Boer-aristocrat. The wedding service was conducted by Pastor Donges, the father of the latter Minister, and it was undoubtedly drawn out, because this minister was known amongst the older generation as an exegete and rationalist. The sermon could be thought out ever so carefully, but Duintjies as he was known by, would easily argue the merits of his own annotations, which resulted in the public worship being stretched to beyond lunch times. Not that anybody held it against him! The old forefathers were a lot more patient with their learned people than they are today.

After the service by ds. Donges, the bridal procession head out to the grand Preller homestead, on their part of Gladdedrif, which they called De Bank. If it rained, it did not dampen the spirit of anybody because the homestead on De Bank was the largest in the whole Onder-Vals. A Frenchman, Emile, and a Hollander, Jan de Wachter, had broken and cut the sandstone into large bricks and sent them to start building the house. But the task was so enormous that after a year they just disappeared. A second builder, Willem Knoetze, took another three years to complete this house, which was burnt down by the British during the Anglo-Boer War. Helletta Lephina, for whom Abraham Preller had built the house for, did not live long enough to see it through to completion. A second wife, with adolescent children, came and died; only a third – young wife, Johanna Wessels – got the heavy hangings and wall paper sent by train from the Cape, served the meals around the enormous walnut tree table and there gave birth to children. Helletta Lephina did her duty with the large abstract oil painting in the lounge.

All the rooms were decorated with anything that was green in the winter months. The young folk crowded around the tables lay with cake, biscuits, milk tart and sugared fruit. The three storied bridal cake was decorated with silver leaves and artistic icing, very luxurious and unusual for that time. The Preller's had ordered the cake from Fichardt in Bloemfontein and had it sent by mail coach from Kroonstad after being railed. The cake had to withstand the rough road and bumpy drifts.

The guests thong in the long, broad passages, the pantry, the living rooms and on the spacious verandah. The young men serve ginger-beer and warm wine-punch, and frolic with the maidens. The bridal couple, together with the older family members and prominent persons from the district sit at the dining room table, with side tables. Here lengthy speeches and toasts are made on both sides of the families, because weddings were one of the important platforms for public speakers in those days; and it was celebrated with very good Cape wines and imported gin. A heavy meal of suckling pig, lambs-pie, yellow rice and steamed potatoes is brought inside. A full-bodied sweet adorns the centre of the table, steaming in its 'witblits' (bootleg), cinnamon, sugar and lemon peels – so intoxicating that's its aroma was enough to take ones breath away.

By the light large, heavy hanging lamps with its glass shades hanging from the broad yellow-wood ceiling, the feast was eaten. They were the people who had tamed the wild tributaries of the Vals River, laid out their church and town, managed it and annually dispatched their council meeting reports to Bloemfontein by coach and horses. They would be welcomed by Cornelis Wessels, waiting for them at the impressive pillars of the Raadsaal – Government Chambers, where they would partake of a presentable meal, and discuss news reports with the smooth advocate Abraham Fischer.

But times were a changing; it would even give way to the most thoughtless. One just had to look at the balmy Italian who dressed himself in a black waiter's suit, with a white cooks-hat, and who dramatically introduced himself in broken Afrikaans as Emilio Castignani. He claims to be the bridegroom's best friend. He serves, he encourages, he praises the aroma of the servings, the ladies clothing, and the men's tobacco. He tells jokes, he approves the weighty hypothesis of the speakers proposing toasts, he hums Italian street music, he murmurs and strikes his hand against his chest and over his heart when there is spoken of the brides brilliant future and how lovely and elegant she looks.

Before the Cape wine began to have its effect there must have been certain guest who took exception to the impudent Italian at such a classy Boer-wedding, and whispered amongst themselves that the foreigners from Kimberley and Johannesburg were infiltrating everywhere.

Kimberley brought in a flood of Uitlanders and loafers in 1871 to the West-Free State with the fever to prospect for anything. Before long the Sandvelders found that Frans de Raedt discovered coal at Vierfontein, and polluted their clean drifts with pitch black coal wagons en route to Kimberley. They had hardly come to accept this when gold was discovered at Johannesburg. Then the fat was in the fire, and this brought in a stream of riff-raff from the North. Everywhere around Klerksdorp little mines sprung up, with miners gallivanting and using God's name in vain in the bars and at the gambling tables.

On a day a prospector is found sitting at the road to Rondebossie, the farm of Jan Steyn, and watches how the ants remove grains just like at Kimberley. Before Jan Steyn could say 'knife', a diamond mine was established on his farm. De Beers pounded on him and bought the ground from under him, and now he is rich Jan Steyn who travels with the boastful span of horses and landau – so whispers the people – ostensibly specially to hire a cart and horses to go to the Cape on 'business'. There in front of the barmaid he lights his pipe with five pound notes.

Near Jan Steyn's mine, Lacemine, were two Italians Renaldo and Cicero Castignani who had a small shop. The Italian who was at the smart Boer-wedding was Emilio, the third brother who had recently emigrated from Italy.

Yes, Lizzie and Jannie Geldenhuys had a distinctly spectacular wedding

But the burghers who had attended the 1899 target–shooting where the Free State government had issued everybody with one hundred mauser bullets, with the strict instruction under no circumstances to use it, and where they got hour long lectures over bodily and head by experienced Majuba-marksmen, could they reach their own conclusions.

The Geldenhuyse would have politely but without interest, listened. According to the journal that Jannie kept later during the War, was his people not unduly locked into the political situation of their time. They would apparently have considered it not “kosher” to trouble such a festive opportunity with insoluble problems.

Dutifully from a front-room they would already see the light prancing of the concertina, and wait their turn to slip out one at a time to join the fray. They all had the English and Boer concertinas, the guitar and the new-fangled banjo which they played, and were fond of dancing. Not just reeling. They were masters of the mazurka and the lancers and knew that a person could in the spaciousness of the De Bank homestead execute such a dance with taste and precision.

Abraham Preller could also hear the concertina, but he stubbornly confined his conversation to land matters. His house, his virtuous house is being subjected to worldly music for the first time in its existence. What could he do but pretend that he could not hear it. He places his hand peremptory on his young wife’s knee so that she would perhaps in her youthful indifference not keep time with the music. It was considerate of him, or so he thought, to build a house for Jannie and Lizzie just across the large homestead, over the depression, because he would keep a firm hand on the rudder. He sees how the groom ushers his bride out the door in the direction of the shriek music.

In the front-room the bridal couple are boisterously welcomed, and everybody stands back so that they could grace the dance-floor. Jannie gallantly takes a bow in front of his wife. His courting is of the highest order; relaxed and charming. He twirls her across the dance floor. He is an accomplished dancer, but he adjusts his footsteps to his clumsy bride. She only knows the steps from hearsay. Her knowledge of music was gained at college – the organ and piano – and the crazes she had learned to play, was church music (she was the church organist of the town up to the time of her marriage, and here and there a popular Victorian hit like "*Over the Waves*", "*Silent Confession*" and "*Whispering Hope*". Sang they did, out of the Sankey and the old "*Globe*" song albums.

The time arrives, after a few dances – everybody knows it. The youngsters look forward to the moment with eagerness; the elderly remind themselves with melancholy. The bridal couple must depart for the nuptial couch. Lizzie is helped to get on top of the round table. Jannie holds her hand. She is blindfolded, and turns in circles. All the single couple's crowd around the table – she has to throw her bouquet for somebody to catch it. For a young girl it is virtually impossible with all the young bachelors with arms outstretched. Young men grab the girls around their waists and hoist them in the air. Even if she does not catch the bouquet, just being held is something. Few of them realised at the privilege of catching the bouquet because it meant surviving the War and still being able to marry.

Lizzie disappears unnoticed, changes out of her wedding dress and meets Jannie at the back door. The light from the kitchen shines on a brand new half-tent carriage with springbuck leather cushions and a brand new harness. Even the pair of brown coach-horses she does not recognise. Everything looked beautiful, exciting and prosperous. A year later she would be pregnant, and flee apprehensively in it from the British army.

They sit close together as the horses set course down the white moonlit track. About a mile from the large house, across a hollow where a few 'katbos' – cat bush – are present stands a four-roomed house which they have already christened "*Katbos View*".

They unlock the front door, and he carries her since time immemorial across the threshold, and lights the candle. Then he returns to stable the horse. She dresses with her printed calico nightgown and heavy embroidery, combs her long white hair and plaits it. He proceeds to the lounge and modestly sits in an easy-chair until she is finished. He takes care that the knotted quilt is properly tucked in around her when she climbed into the feather-bed, because he loves her and would always in future ensure that she is protected.

And if there was a search light in every window of the big house, or the continuous rain dripped though a hole onto the floor smeared with cow-dung, or whether this was said in Pretoria, or that in Bloemfontein, the love in Katbos View was young and sweet and enough for a life time together.

Oumam Lizzie's Book

25th September 1899. Oudad Jan received a letter from his father-in-law Preller, to report urgently to hear what tidings Commandant Felie Nel brought from President Steyn. The Free State and Transvaal were ordered to prepare for war since Lord Kitchener had boarded ship with 10,000 troops bound for South Africa. In view of the drastic tidings, Oumam Lizzie was advised to seek shelter with Oudad Jan's parents on their farm, Rietgat, about twenty five miles from Bothaville towards Kroonstad.

Preparations on made on Friday 1st October to take the wagon drawn by six horses, to Kroonstad in order to attend the *nagmaal* - Holy Communion on the Sunday. And what a day it turned out to be, with war declared in the morning during the church service. "All arms-bearing men-folk are called up for military service: they are to with saddled horses, rifle, one blanket and own rations for three days".

All the womenfolk are engaged in baking bread, making rusks, packing biltong (dried strips of beef) and helping the men get ready to go to war.

Oudad Jan's Diary

My grandfather, Johannes Albertus Geldenhuys, affectionately called 'Oudad Jan or Jannie, commenced his diaries as follows:-

On the evening of **3rd October 1899** my father Hendrik Jacobus Geldenhuys and I were commandeered to be present the next day on the farm De Rust of Veldcornet Gert Pieterse. During the day there was much slaughtering of livestock and baking bread and biscuits by our relatives. As expected everyone was broken-hearted to bid "Afskeid neem" – bidding 'good-bye' as dramatically depicted by the sculpture in front of the Anglo–Boer War Museum in Bloemfontein. Our loved ones did not know whether we would see each other again on this earth. We left early morning the next day and arrived at De Rust to find many other Burgers already assembled there.

A krygsraad or war-council was held and it was decided that Commandant Nel and the 'Upper constituency' (Upper constituency of Kroonstad. Onder Vaal was the Bothaville district or Commando) should deploy to the Natal border; while Mister Martinus Schoeman was chosen as Commandant to go with us to Kimberley. My father was chosen as Assistant Veldcornet to Karel Coetzee. Coetzee appointed me as his 'pen-master' scribe or Secretary. My brother Pieter accompanied me in our half-tent ox-wagon drawn by eight oxen. We formed up in one very large Commando. There is much whip-lashing with ox-hide to get the convoy moving to the Western Front.

'Afskeid' - Bidding farewell

We travelled through Bultfontein and that night I developed painful toothache. Early the next morning I had Dr Groenewald extract the tooth. We carried on past Boshof but when we got to Louwfonteyn our Commandant received orders to take a horse-commando / cavalry ahead while the laager followed behind. We proceeded to nearby Olifantsfontein where we found a much larger laager under command of Chief Commandant Cornelis Hermanus Wessels. Olifantsfontein became the main burger larger, which besieged Kimberley. It featured very prominently during the Western Front campaign in respect of treatment of sick and wounded, hospitalisation, weaponry and war supplies.

Our commando is divided with one half going to Scholtznek and the other to Armoeds Kopje. These two hills straddled the railway line into Kimberley, where Pieter and I were sent.

We spent a miserable cold night with only one rain-coat each to serve as bedding on uncomfortable sharp rocks. Our horses were tethered to trees on the southern slopes of the hill. Watch is kept during the night, but hidden from the Kimberley search lights as they swept from one side to the other.

Kimberley Search-light – used to signal to Methuen's column

At dawn we returned to the main laager at Olifantsfontein, in time to see the arrival of our own laager. We had had nothing to eat since the previous day and took delight in having a hearty meal.

Pieter and I then made a plan to return to Scholtznek and were informed by Veldcornet Pieterse that they had ambushed an armoured train from Kimberley, which then beat a very hasty retreat from where it had come.

The rail route was focal to the British advance, and relief of Kimberley. Cecil John Rhodes, who was resident in Kimberley during the duration of the siege, had his mine engineer George Labram armour-plate the trains that carried out forages north and south of the diamond down. Kevin Ritchie, the managing editor of the Diamond Fields Advertise had this to say in May 2000: "Had it not been for diamonds and Cecil Rhodes, Kimberley might never have been besieged and the British would never have had to expend so much time, so many lives and so much money fighting all the way up the railway line to get there."

We did not stay long and was sent back to Armoeds Kopje – which was later named Schoeman's Fort, after our Commandant, and instructed to ensure that nobody entered or left Kimberley. The town is bombarded from the south to which the English returned fire. About mid-November one Commando was sent to the Groot River (Orange River) and returned with the news that Lord Methuen was massing a large army destined for the relief of Kimberley.

The Burgers at Armoeds Kopje are ordered to saddle up the best horses in single file, to accompany the Commando's counter-attack in the south. By this time we were joined by our brother-in-law Charlie [Preller]. Because we had become sick and tired of Armoeds Kopje, we readily volunteered to go on the offensive. While preparing at Olifantsfontein, 'Raadslid' [government member] Hendrik Serfontein is chosen as Veldcornet to go with us.

Schoeman was ill and thus could not come along. Barend Greyling was chosen in lieu of Veldcornet Gert Pieterse. Assistant Veldcornet Karel Coetzee, under whom I served, had no excuse and had to go as well. Charlie, Pieter and Van der Berg and I went with our weapons. We had our own domestic servants, and hindered no one. We had a cook who looked after the wagon and another to care for the horses. We had ample rusks, cakes and tinned meat, slept on feathered beds and lived like "Lords". We proceeded to Rooidam close to Belmont, left our laager behind and by horseback took up positions in the hills around Belmont.

The first action occurred on 9th November when Kommandant van der Merwe's commando had a skirmish with Colonel Gough's two squadrons of the 9th Lancers – losing Lt Col Keith Falconer killed and Lt Wood fatally wounded. Lord Methuen arrived on the 12th to take over command of the British forces. Minor clashes occurred on the 21st and 22nd while Lt-General Methuen moved his forces 19 km from the Orange River Station.

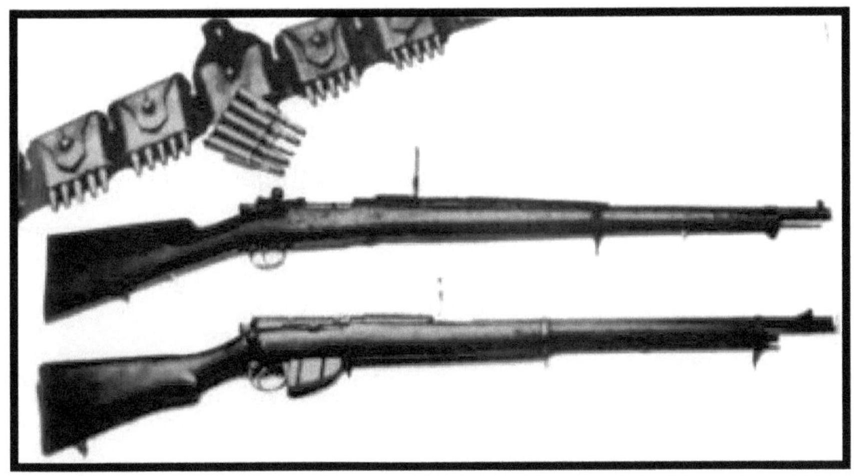

Mauzer and Lee-Metford rifles

We soon spotted thousands of soldiers following the line of rail on the **22nd November** and at about midday we were dispatched by Coetzee and Greyling to destroy the railway line, starting from Belmont station. We obtained hammers, picks and other necessary tools and set about the task in high spirits – like playing cats and mice! There is not much at the actual siding – but the surrounding terrain is fascinating. To the south-west of the rail and road is Finchams' Farm, surrounded by hills, with plenty of water - a green oasis in the wilderness of an arid Karoo. To the east are two prominent hill features – Vernier and Gun Hills – the obvious choice for the Boers who would have commanding views over the valley floor leading to the Orange River Station. And from where the British movements would be spotted while maintaining their own invisibility – and thus element of surprise – so essential from a principle of war is concerned.

Whilst we busied ourselves demolishing the railway we noted a group of soldiers at a kraal about 2100 yards distant. It did not take long before we were fired on by Lee-Metford rifles and were obliged to seek shelter in the nearby hills, while Major Albrecht opened up on the enemy with artillery fire, in the afternoon. As soon as our bombardment ceased, the enemy bombarded us with a large number of cannons. The bombardment continued till well after dark with us losing a couple of burgers killed and wounded. We expected a night assault and at 2am on **23rd November** Veldcornet Greyling led us to another position. Fifteen minutes later the enemy stormed the position we had vacated, and sent down such a barrage as to resonate though out the mountains. The cannon fire stopped as soon as it became light, but was soon replaced by small arms fire. These actions precipitated the Battle of Belmont, with the British forces storming the Boer strongholds.

The Battle grounds at Belmont

At 7 pm Pieter's (Oudad's brother) horse got shot, while still holding his position. The Burger and I withdrew and pleaded to Pieter to 'make a plan'. I mounted my horse and waited till the last moment in order for Pieter to make good his escape. As I galloped through a hail of cannon and gun-fire, my horse was shot in a front-leg – at about 800 paces from the enemy. Having arrived at the Commandant's position, I joined burger Paarman, but my horse wandered off to graze. I was thus forced to retrieve it but in the process the horse is shot in its rump with a third fatal in the saddle flap. My horse stumbles and falls while I entertain thoughts of securing my own safety.

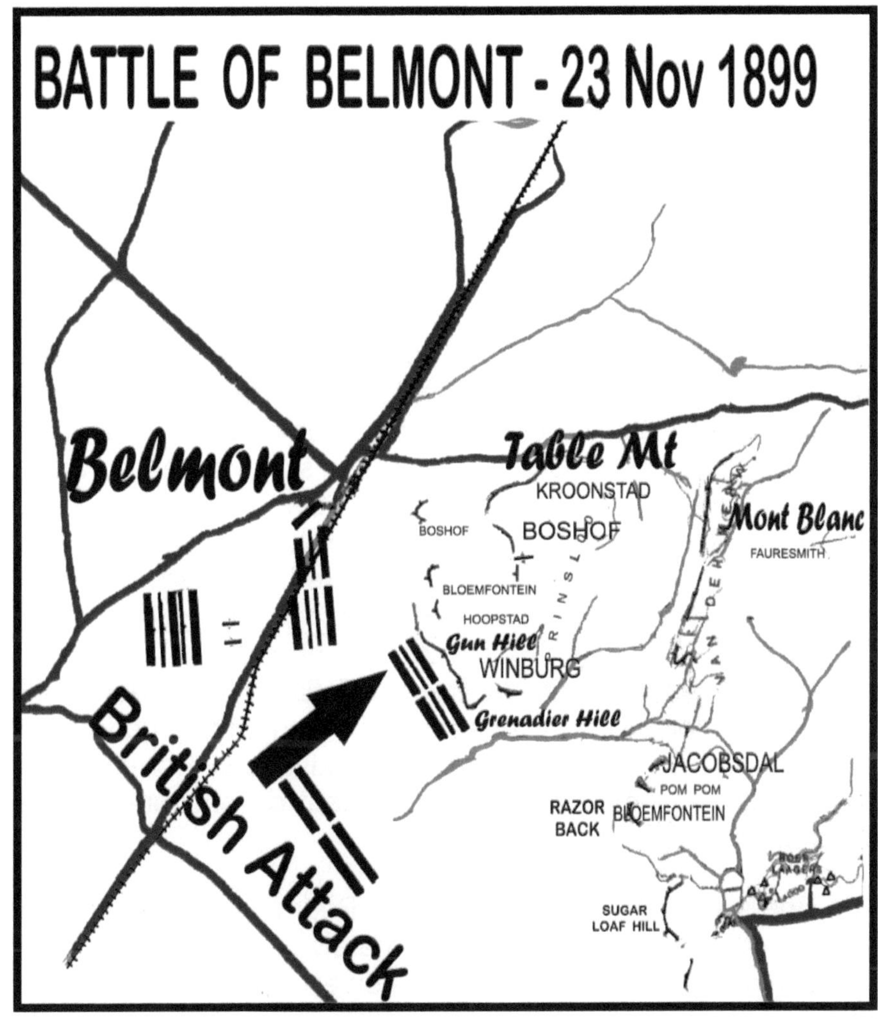

Battle of Belmont - 23 November 1899

However, I could not abandon my saddle on the battlefield; I cut it loose and carried it away to safety. Just as I became exhausted I met up with Pieter who then helped me carry it till 1 pm when we came upon the Fouriesmith Commando who helped us find our own laager. It was dreadful to meet up with our dead and wounded Burgers – many praying and pleading for help. Not having had anything to eat the whole day it was a great relief to have our first meal. We briefed our laager that our horses died on the Belmont battlefield.

The Boers, mainly Free Staters, had less than a hundred casualties, whereas the British suffered over 300 dead, wounded and missing – which included General Featherstonhaugh. Boer General Prinsloo withdrew his commandos the 21 kilometres east to Ramdam, across the Free State border.

On the **25th November** we took up ambush and defensive positions on the farm called Graspan or Rooilaagte. The battle raged from early morning till late afternoon. Dr Jackie Grobler reports that numerous Free State burghers were dissatisfied with the leadership of Chief Commandant Jacobus Prinsloo, with some demanding leave to return to their farms. Some simply left the front. General Koos de la Rey arrived with 600 men to restore morale and to command the Battle of Graspan - 25 November 1899. The Boers then numbered barely 2000, pitted against Khaki General Methuen's much larger army. However, the Burgers were outnumbered and forced to withdraw while the enemy advanced slowly towards Kimberley. At six o'clock on the 25th, the Boers fired one shot with their Krupp gun on a British armoured train, but missed the target. The British retaliated with a bombardment and mounted troops attempted to outflank De la Rey's left flank. The Fauresmith Commando, joined by Jacobsdal Commando, managed to halt and temporary contain the British advance. Commandant Lubbe was wounded in the eye but kept on encouraging the burghers to defend their positions.

The Boers lost 20 killed including pro-Boer millionaire Uitlander Jeppe, 40 wounded and approximately 25 taken prisoners. Once again the Boers suffered fewer casualties than the British.

At the Battle of Enslin the British continued to follow the same tactics of a heavy artillery bombardment followed by a frontal infantry attack, and again it resulted in a Boer retreat at the cost of heavy British casualties. The action lasted some six hours, with the Boers making good their escape during the hours of darkness. The Brits were thus able to advance on to Klokfontein – being within striking distance of Modder River, as well as having the advantage of an adequate supply of water for men and beast.

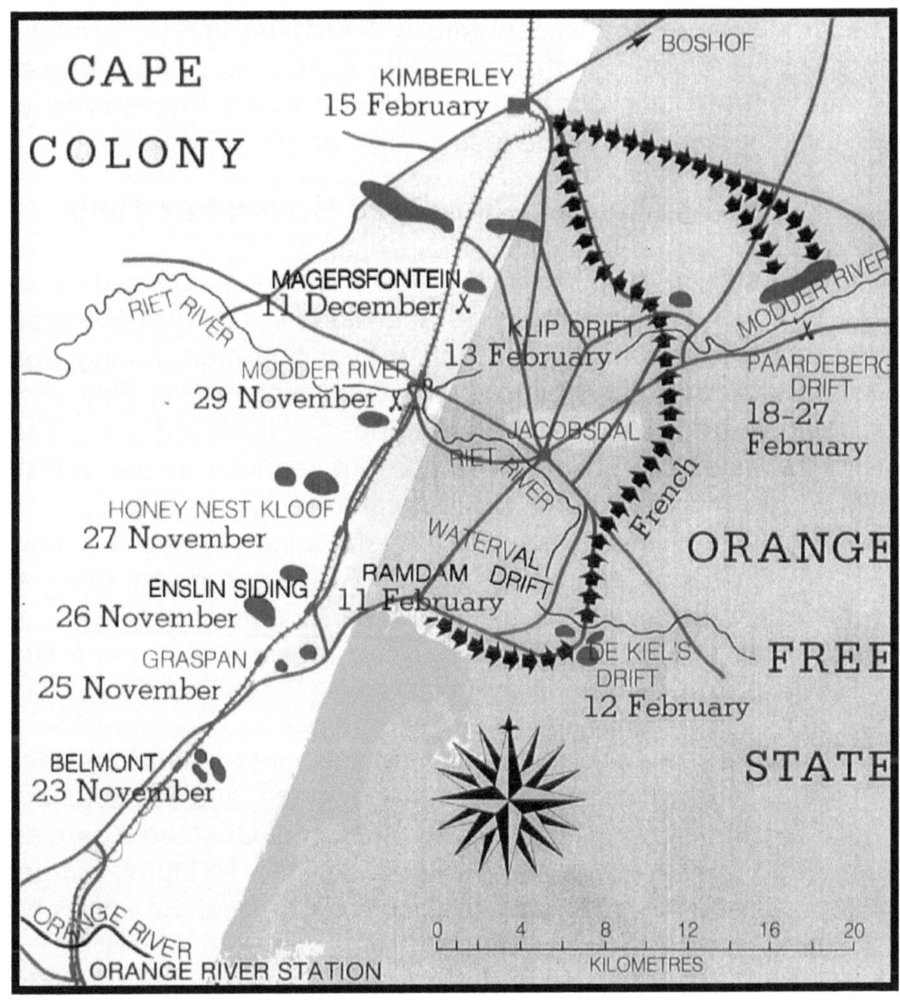

Western Front battle map. Cape Colony and Orange Free State border

On the **27th November** we took up defensive positions at Twee Rivers [Modder and Riet Rivers - General Piet Cronjé arrived too late from Mafeking, to take over overall command of the Western Front.], where heavy fighting took place, with large losses inflicted on the enemy [the Battle raged all day, in temperatures that were measured at 43°C – with the Boers fortunately having some shade and water from the rivers]. Despite this, we abandoned our positions when night fell, and took up defences at Magersfontein Mountain. Our Commandant Serfontein was taken prisoner at the earlier Battle of Belmont. Veldcornet Coetzee was wounded above the hip. Veldcornet Greyling received a flesh wound to his head and was sent to the hospital at Jacobsdal. Our wagon thus became without any officers and C. Rensburg and P. Terblans are chosen as our new officers. The night before the Battle of Magersfontein our officers got lost and found themselves at Olifantsfontein. That is the last we saw or heard from them.

Battle of the Modder River – 28 November 1899

At the Battle of Modder River, also sometimes referred to as the Battle of Tweeriviere – Riet and Modder, General Methuen suffered a reversal with the loss of over 500 men, mainly due to the brilliant tactic employed by Gen. Koos de la Rey – of digging in the Boers along the top edges of the riverbanks. The shallow trajectory of the Boer rifle fire resulted in the British falling like ninepins. The Boers withdrew during the night to take up defensive positions at Magersfontein. It was a hollow victory for the British, despite, de la Reys' son being killed at Modder River. He was wounded at Modder river, died at Jacobsdal, and buried at the Burgher Monument – some five kilometres north-east of Magersfontein.

Oudad Jan Geldenhuys' OFS Commando was leaderless after Veldcornet Greyling received a head graze and went to the Jacobsdal hospital for treatment. Veldcornet Coetzee was also wounded. Their replacements, Rensburg and Terblans, did not last long and were in turn replaced by Barend Schutte and Frederick Nel .

Oudad Jan's laager retreated from Modder River to Magersfontein to prepare fortification.

Schalk W. Meintjies is chosen as Commandant of the Kroonstad Commando with Barend Schutte and Frederick Nel as Veldcornets. Our wagon laager joins the main laager at Olifantsfontein.

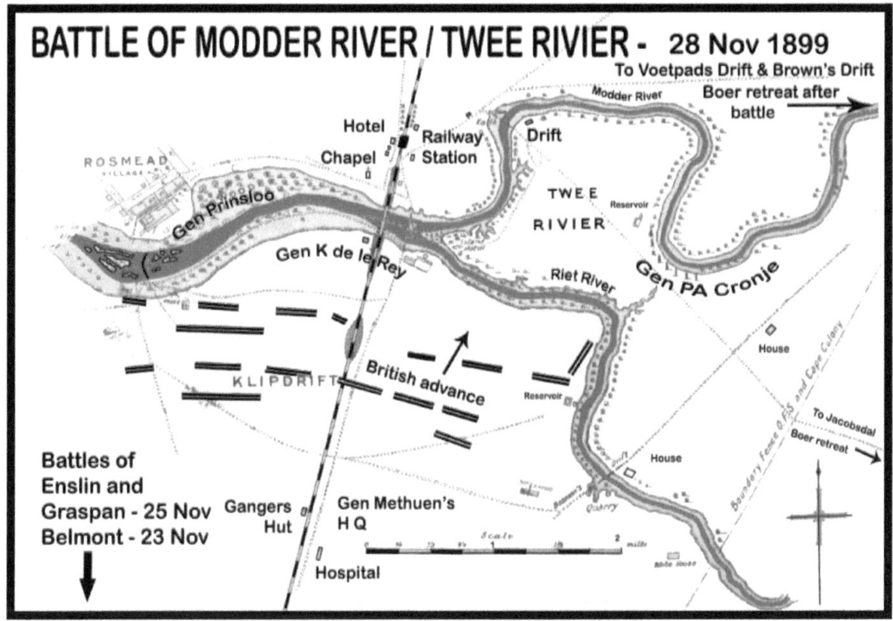

On **10th December** the Commandant ordered me to take a wagon to the main laager to fetch ammunition and provisions. While preparing to leave, and while our natives were harnessing the oxen, the enemy started firing their cannons at us. I left my defensive position at about one o'clock. After dark I proceeded with the wagon and stopped over-night at a farm whose name escapes me.

The Kroonstad Commando was split into three sections – with one section being on the Boers extreme right flank below Langeberg under Andries Cronje; the second section under Piet Cronje immediately below Magerfontein Kop; and with the third platoon part of the O.F.S. Commando's just east of Magerfontein Kop and along the left flank (near the Bloemhof and Lichtenburg commandos commanded by de la Rey).

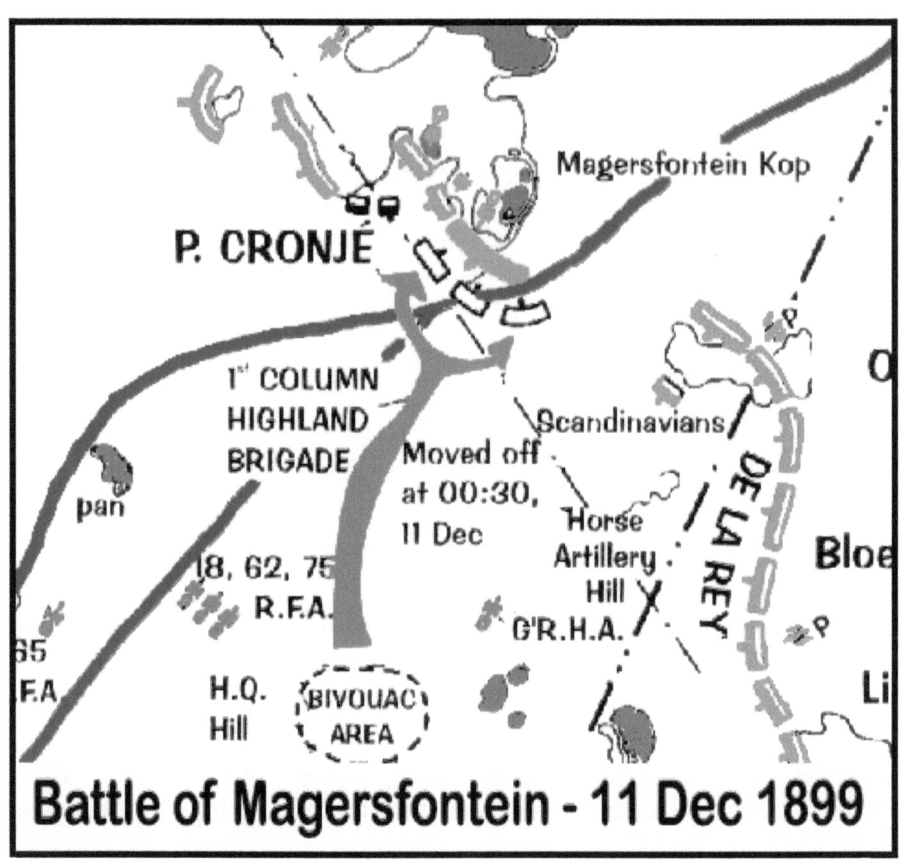

Battle of Magersfontein - 11 Dec 1899

MAGERSFONTEIN

11 December 1899

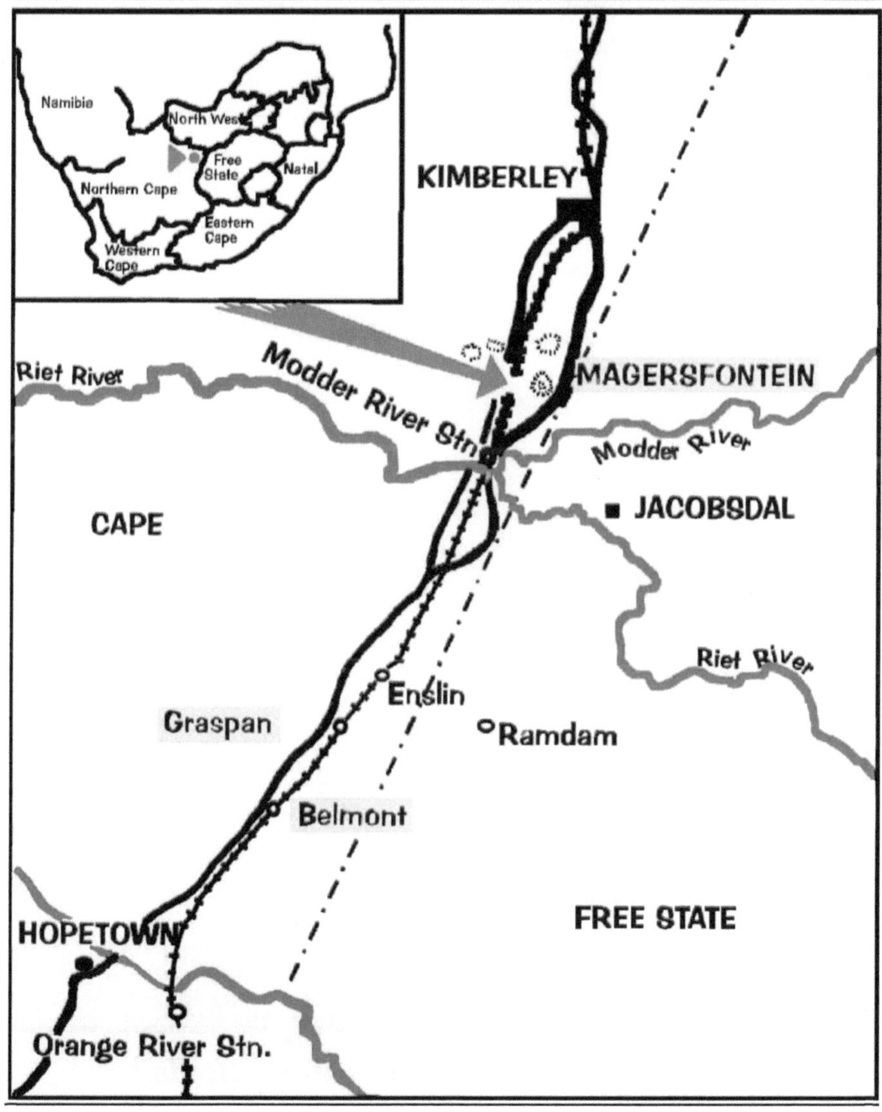

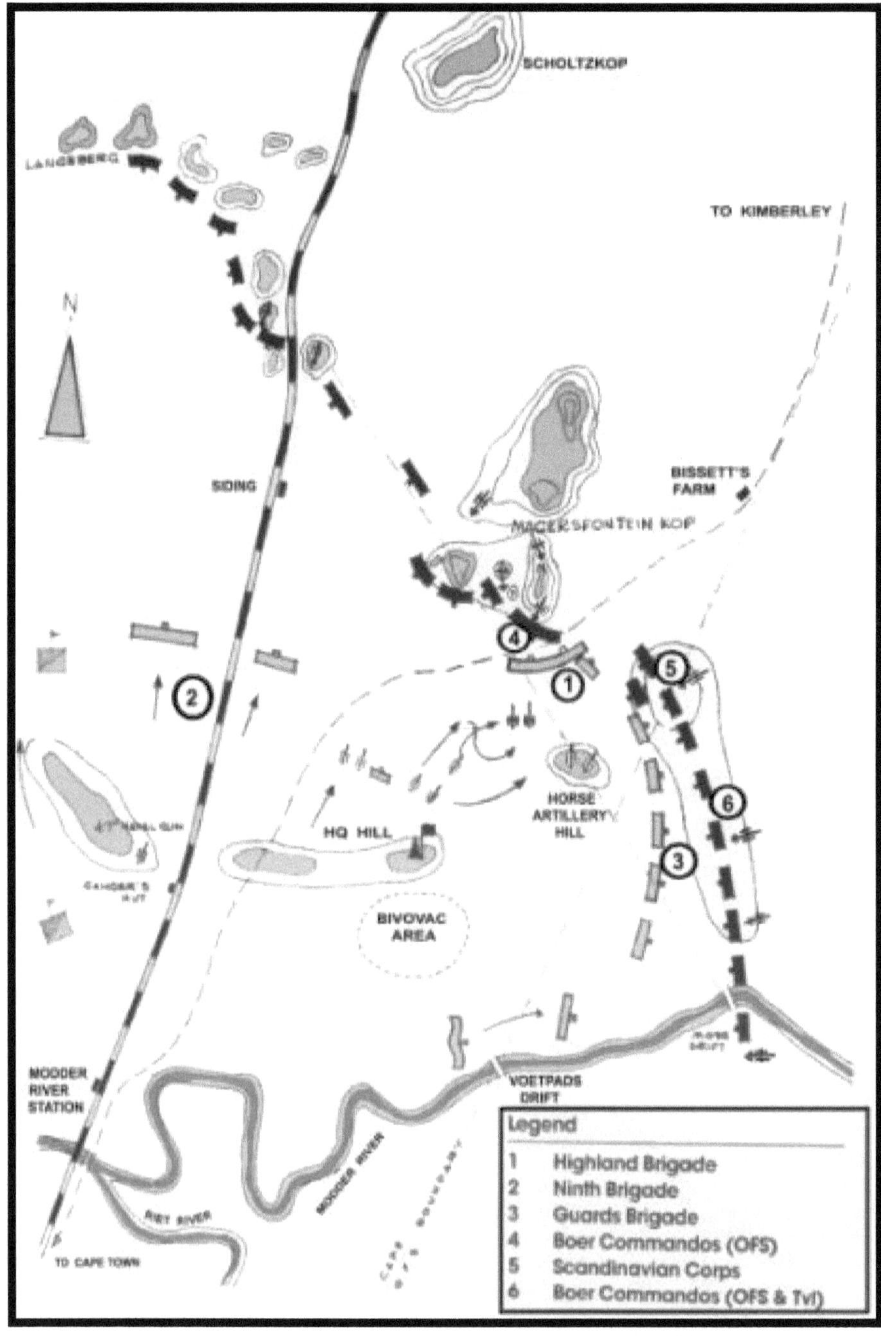

Opposing force positions at Magersfontein

Battle of Magersfontein - 11 December 1899

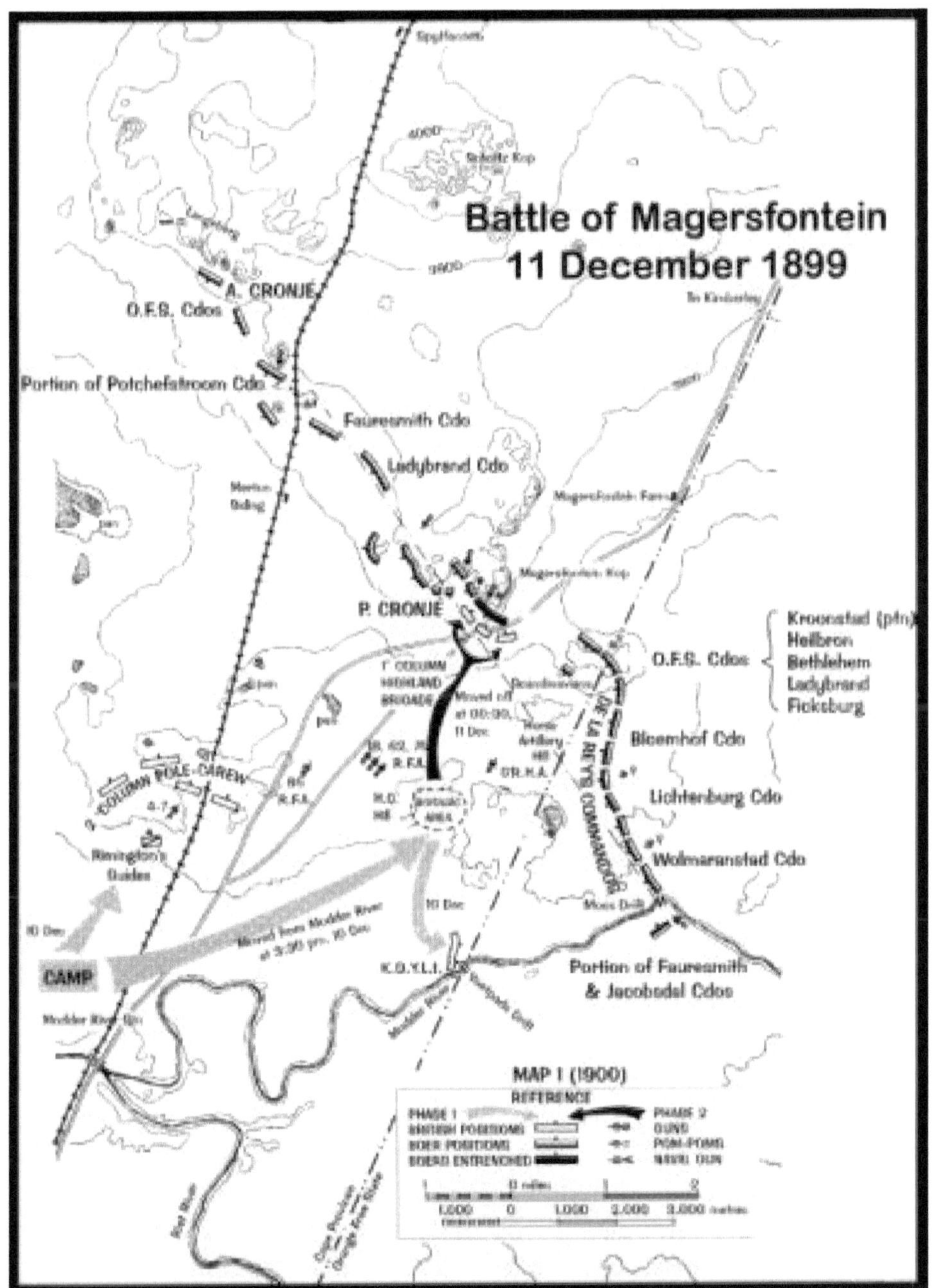

Burgher Monument – some five kilometres north-east of Magersfontein

On the morning of **11th December** I was woke at dawn. Wide spread gunfire signified the start of battle, with cannon firing joining the fray at sunrise. I continued to the main laager at that evening where reports came in that about 200 of our burgers were killed in the battle and our own Veldcornet Meintjies having been wounded, but not seriously. I stayed in the laager three days to get all the necessary provisions and returned to Magersfontein. It was one pitiful sight to see the battlefield with the dead and dying. The enemy casualties were too great for us burgers to bury them all. I was still the secretary to the officers because they were not too proficient with writing. The English had withdrawn to Twee Riviere. Chief Commandant Cornelis Wessels resigned his command and was replaced by Ignatius Ferreira. Our defences at Magersfontein consisted of trenches which we dug, four feet deep and two feet wide. During the night we made the trenches our home. After the Battle of Magersfontein the enemy continued to bombard us by day and night – but used Luddite cannon-shells at night.

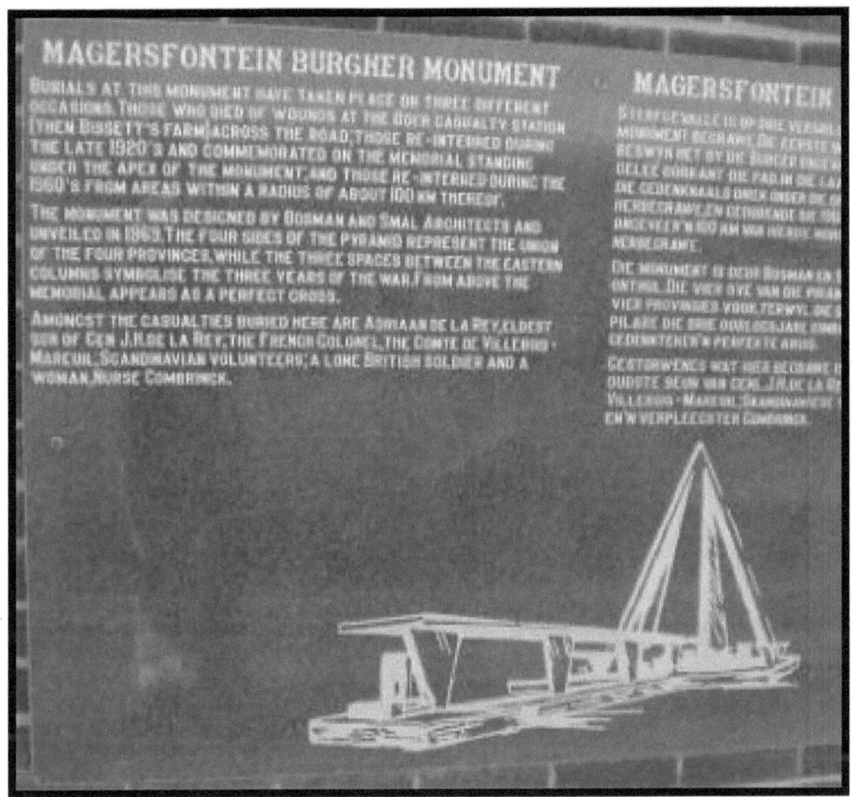

Andy Wauchope who commanded and led the British assault, was struck down within the opening moments. My grandmother records that the Major General fell a mere 14 paces from the Kroonstad Commando trenches – mortally wounded and destined to die moments later. The British casualties numbered over 1000; the Boers had lost 250. The mighty British army was stopped in its tracks by a brilliantly fought battle by the Boers. Every Afrikaner needs to do a pilgrimage to this battle ground, at least once, during their lifetimes. It was a very profound, awe inspiring time, to stand at the well preserved viewing platform and to cast one's gaze towards Modder River.

Battle of Magersfontein

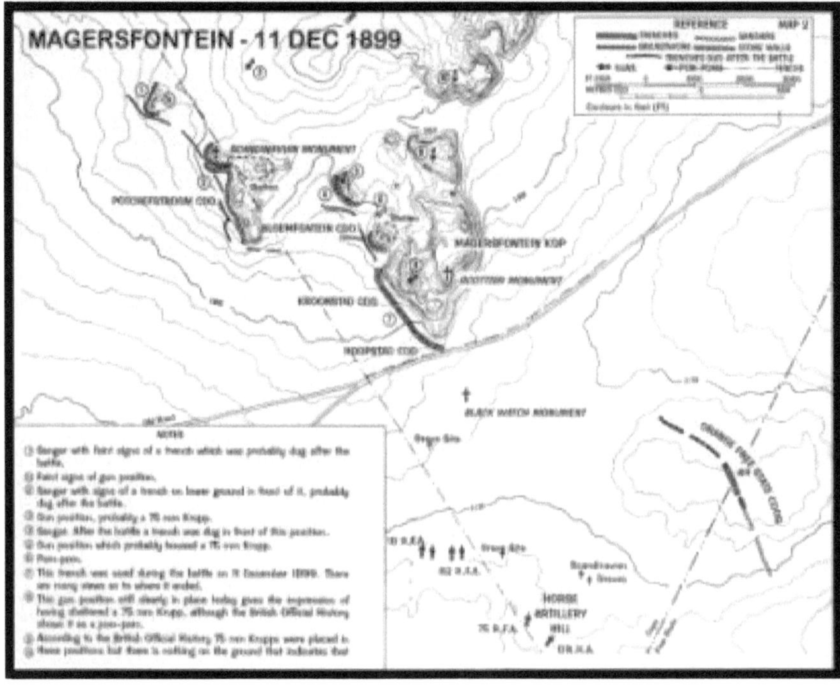

View from top of Magersfontein, towards Modder River

The Black Watch advance just before dawn

The war memorial where General Andy Wauchope fell

The Year 1900

With the arrival of New Year, I was granted two-days leave to return to the laager to visit family, friends, uncles and cousins. Pieter was still stationed at Armoeds Kopje. The New Year passed sadly for us – our dinner consisted of 'vetkoek' and meat. After my leave was over I returned to Magersfontein.

On **21st January** I again was granted leave to go to the main laager to get clean clothing. I arrived at the laager at midday and to my great surprise I met my father who had come to enquire of Pieter and me. We were pleased to hear that my wife and other remaining family members were well. My father informed me that my wife had arranged to send a substitute named Christiaan Grobler, at a cost of one cow with calf per month, as long as the war lasted. I immediately approached Commandant S Pieterse standing in for Commandant Schoeman, and apprised him of the situation. I was referred to Head Commandant Ferreira who approved my substitute and granted me leave of absence to return to my home.

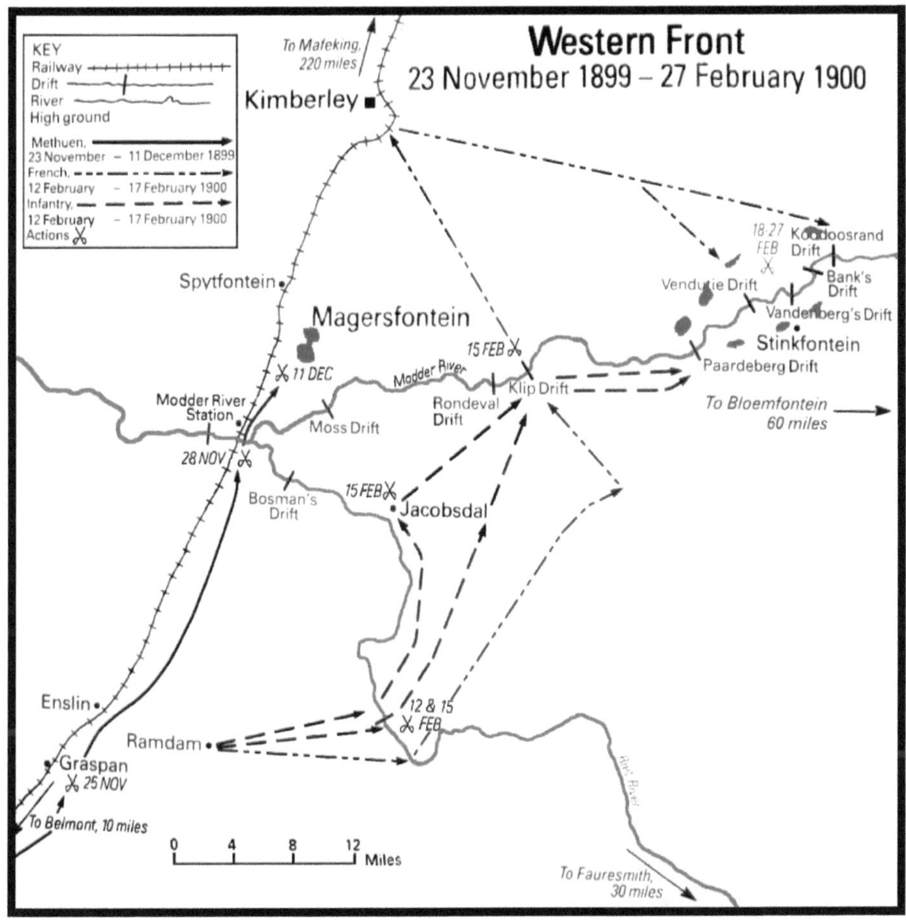

Lord Roberts cleverly bypassed the Boer stronghold at Magersfontein, and thus sped to Kimberley and relieve the siege, much to the relief of Cecil John Rhodes (the founder of Rhodesia)

My father also appealed to him to grant my brother Pieter 15 days leave as he would substitute for him for the full period till he returned. The request was granted and that same afternoon at 3 pm Pieter and I in-spanned one car with six oxen, four mules and two horses and departed in great haste so as not to waste any valuable time. Our journey took three days with us arriving at De Bank at 3 o'clock in the morning. My father-in-law (Abram Preller) and all the children are relieved and glad to welcome us back. More so because so many lives were in danger and during our journey we had overturned the wagon a few times, and had to spend a night near Nervier at Hoopstad because we could not fjord the river. We had to wait till the morning to get the car across by boat while the horses and mules had to swim across.

Our horses were very tired and my father-in-law Abram told me that my wife had gone to Rietgat to visit my mother. My father-in-law gave me his two brown horses to continue the journey, which Pieter and I did soon after breakfast. We arrived at Rietgat about 1 pm, Oh and what an indescribable meeting I had with my dear wife Lizzie. We had been separated for 3 months and 20 days. I stayed behind while Pieter returned to the Commando after his leave had expired.

The rapid British advance had been halted at Magerfontein. Cecil John Rhodes, who was under Boer siege in Kimberley, was hopping mad at the slow British progress. His frustration had to endure well over a week – till General French by-passed the Boer defences and managed his breakthrough to Kimberley. This, then, resulted in most of the Free State burghers assembling in the Paardeberg area – which was the most direct route to their Capital, Bloemfontein.

Paardeberg Tragedy – 20 to 27th February 1900

After General French relieved Kimberley, he successfully intercepted General Cronje, who had laagered some distance upstream along the Modder River, at Wolveskraal. Lord Roberts had taken ill and Kitchener assumed control of the British forces. With Cronje being quickly surrounded, he fought delaying tactics and withstood terrific artillery pounding for nearly ten days. General de Wet came to Cronje's' rescue, and offered an opportunity to escape south across the river. Danie Theron had managed to crawl through the British cordon – and repeated his heroic performance by returning unscathed to de Wet – with the message that the bulk of Cronje's Kommandante had voted not to abandon the women and children – and then surrendered to Roberts. The loss of some four thousand Boers was a terrible blow to Boer morale – in fact it was the turning point in the Boer War.

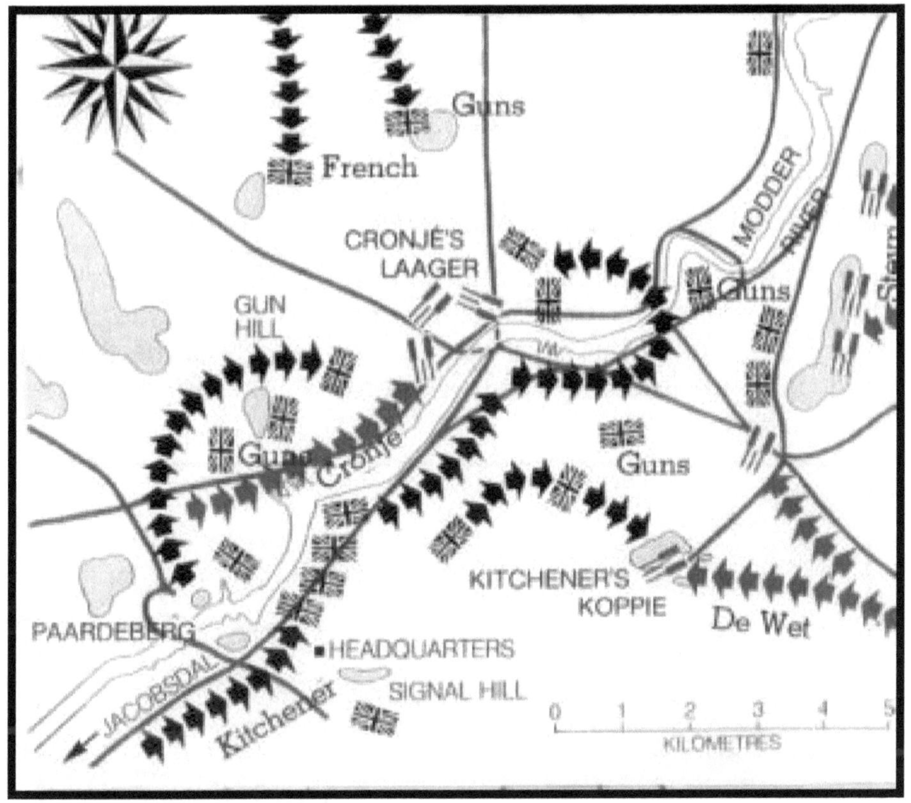

Map showing the opposing forces at the Battle of Paardekraal, where General Cronje surrendered to Lord Roberts

Poplar Grove – and subsequent battle of Abramskraal – 9 March to 10 March 1900. Chief Commandant General de Wet was repulsed at Popular Grove, where Presidents Paul Kruger of the Transvaal and Martinus Steyn of the Free State narrowly escaped being surrounded by the Khakis. The Boers then fell back to Abramskraal, about 66 miles west of Bloemfontein, where a fierce battle was fought along a 20 Kilometre front from north to south. The attacking forces numbered 30 000 soldiers with 30 guns, against 3000 burghers. British cavalry units were checked at Damvlei, while de Wet repulsed Khakis at Driefontein (south west of Damvlei). The positions were valiantly held all day, but were forced to abandon them by six in the evening, having run out of ammunition – for the loss of 30 men killed, 20 captured and 47 wounded. The British appeared to have lost at least 60 killed and 360 wounded.

The magnificent rock skanse are still standing 105 years after the event – and requires binoculars to appreciate how well the

Boers were in fact camouflaged amongst the rocky outcrops. It is rumoured that Kruger was forced to use his shambok to exhort the Boers not to surrender so easily to Lord Roberts' killing machine. However, despite this last bastion the Boers gave hardly any resistance.

Oudad Jan Geldenhuys continues with his diary entry:

My father HJ Geldenhuys returned on **2nd May (1900).** After I had been home for three months our healthy daughter Hettie was born. During this time we received reports of the fighting, and that in February how General P Cronje had been surrounded.

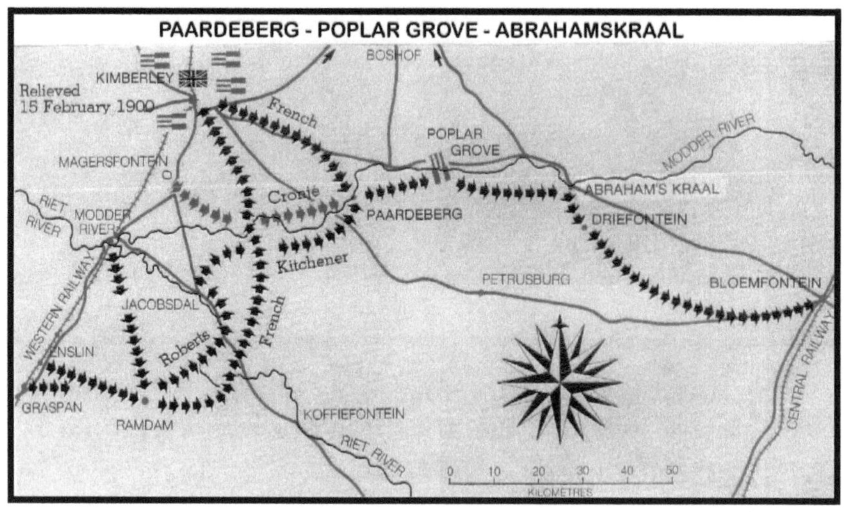

The ten day Battle of Paardeberg with the surrender of 4000 burghers and loss of 400 wagons was the turning point in the Anglo-Boer war. Cronje had put up a gallant defence – but the effect was demoralising to the vast majority of Free Staters. – and eventually surrendered with a large number of Burgers, with the enemy heading to Bloemfontein. When Bloemfontein (Bloemfontein was occupied on the 16th March 1900. The Free State capital then moved to Kroonstad – after rousing speeches at the Sand River (and pointing out British treachery following the betrayal of the Sand River Convention of 1852) fell to the enemy, the Burgers became demoralised and many returned to their homes. Lord Roberts issued a Proclamation for the Burgers to lay down their arms. Our Commando, from the Lower (Onder) Valsch River thus went home and waited for the enemy to appear because the situation now appeared hopeless.

Sangars at Abramskraal

Abram Carl Preller's brother, and father to historian Dr Gustav Preller – Commandant Robbie Clunie Preller, was meanwhile supporting General Stephanus Schoeman on the Southern Front – at Colesberg. At about this time, the Boer forces was considerably reduced when de le Rey, and Schoeman, was summoned to assist with the defence of Bloemfontein. De le Rey appointed General H R Lemmer as provisional Chief Commandant for the Southern front – which upset Robbie Preller terribly, because Schoeman was not prepared to accept Lemmer's appointment as commander in his place. Preller, who was Schoeman's brother-in-law, was found guilty of stirring up feelings against Lemmer, discharged and sent back to Pretoria. Schoeman then refused to carry out his orders to send back deserters to the Transvaal front, and also returned to Pretoria. Preller later returned to Colesberg – was wounded, captured on the 7 September 1901, as sent to Shajahanpur in India.

Bloemfontein, the Free State capital fell on 13th March, Kroonstad on 12th May 1900. Many Free Stater Boers returned to their farms.

On the **24th May** Lord Methuen trekked into Bothaville with his column. We surrendered our weapons and took an Oath of Neutrality. Father-in-law Abram is taken Prisoner-of-War to Kroonstad with the Column – by Order of the English authorities to detain all Officers (he was still Veldcornet in lieu of Veldcornet Karel Coetzee). It was a sad parting to which we could do nothing. He was detained for a month and released to return peacefully to his home.

Authors note: A section of Oudad's diary is missing. Inserted in lieu is additional research conducted that readers may find appropriate. General Frederik Albertus Grobler, who commanded the Waterberg and Zoutpansberg commandos, was ordered to attack Fort Tuli and then destroy the railway right up to Bulawayo. Pretoria was concerned in the "probability that the English would come via Beira", rail down to relieve Mafeking and march onto the Boer capital (lessons learnt from the ill-fated January 1896 Dr. L.S. Jameson raid). This Gen. Grobler failed to do – and permitted the Rhodesians under Lt.-Col. H.C.O. Plumer to secure the railway initially up to Gaberone and subsequently to Ramathlabama (just north of Mafeking). Plumer was reinforced by Canadians and New Zealanders (via Beira, Zeedeberg stagecoach, and Bulawayo line of rail – as originally feared by the Boer High Command). Plumer joined up with Colonel Bryan T. Mahon – Lord Robert's specially appointed Flying Column, and they both successfully relieved General Robert S.S. Baden-Powell in Mafeking on 17th May 1900.

A Lotter also featured during the declaration of hostilities during the Anglo-Boer War. It is known that he, together with Scheepers, Kritzinger and Malan operated south of the Orange River, in the Colesberg – Noupoort district. (As opposed to de Wet in the Free State; Botha, Beyers and Viljoen in ZAR/Transvaal, de le Rey / Kemp in Klerksdorp – Mafeking area; and Maritz / Jannie Smuts in north-western Cape). Further research will be needed to establish his contribution to the outcomes of history.

According to the *Malan-gedenkboek*, page 53, a Komdt Hercules Philip Malan, born 2nd November 1836, died on 2nd December 1899 during the war. General Wynand Charl Malan, born 16th August 1872, from Beyersfontein, Murraysburg, was also a famous Boer general, who went to Tanganyika in 1907.

Komdt Abram Hugo Malan, 14th child of Carel Wynand and Magdalena Hugo, married Hendrina Joubert, daughter of Boer General Piet Joubert.

Robert Clunie Logie Preller (born 5th May 1846, the fourth son and seventh child of Carel Frederik) had married Stephanie Maria Aletta Schoeman – daughter of Kommandant-General Stephanus Schoeman. During the war he fought the Brits on the Colesberg, southern front. I should mention that he served with distinction in the Colesberg and Philippolis areas and is quoted extensively by Professor Fransjohan Pretorius, historian at the University of Pretoria, in his "*Kommandolewe Tydens die Anglo-Boereoorlog 1899-1902*", which was published by Human and Rousseau in 1991.

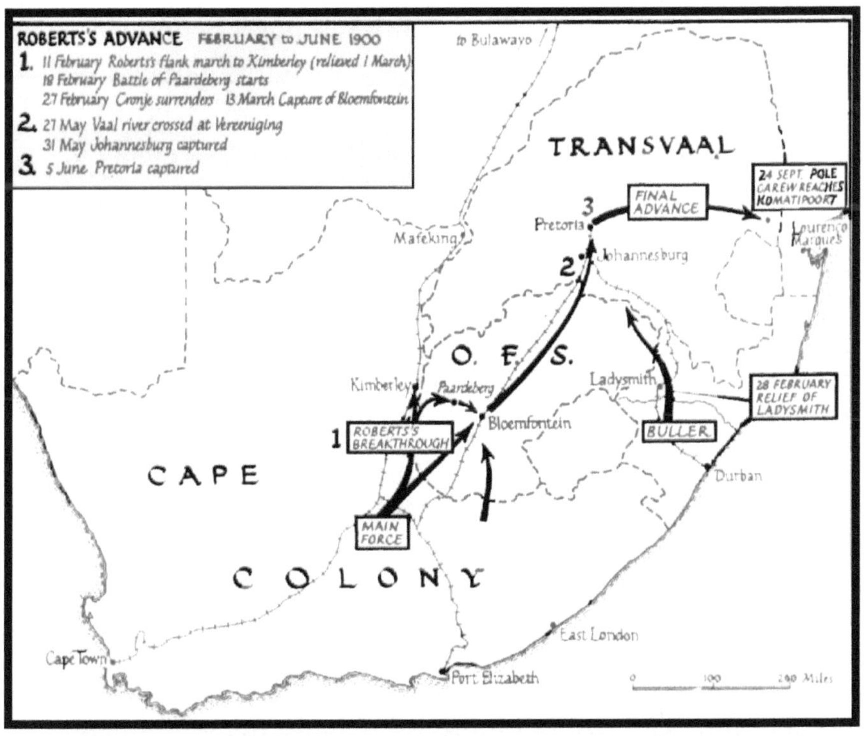

The map illustrates Lord Robert's rapid advance to Pretoria, after the Boers capitulated at Paardeberg

General CR de Wet wrote in his "*Three Years War*" about Thring as follows: . . . At Kroonstad there was not a single burgher left. Only the inhabitants of the township remained, and they were too ready to "hands-up." One of these, however, was of a different mould. I refer to Veldcornet Thring, who had arrived with me at Kroonstad that morning, but who had suddenly fallen ill. On the day following he was a prisoner in the hands of the English. Thring was an honourable man in every way. Although an Englishman by birth, he was at heart an Afrikaner, for he had accepted the Orange Free State as his second fatherland. Like many other Englishman, he had become a fellow-citizen of ours, and had enjoyed the fat of the land. But now, trusty burgher that he was, he had drawn his sword to defend the burgher's rights. His earliest experiences were with the Kroonstad burgers, who went down into Natal (fought at Ladysmith); later on he fought under me at Sanna's Post (sabotaging the Bloemfontein water works and supply), and Mostertshoek, and took part in the siege of Colonel Dalgety at Jammersbergsdrift. He had stood at my side at Thaba'Nchu and on the banks of the Zand River (Sand River). I had always found him the most willing and reliable of officers, and he had won the respect and trust of every man who knew him." Now that was quite a praiseworthy commendation coming from the famous General!

A. Lester Thring wrote an unpublished manuscript titled "*Seven Months on commando under Commandant Prinsloo and General De Wet*". He is mentioned briefly in Pretoria University historian Prof. Fransjohan Pretorius' "*Kommandolewe tydens die Anglo-Boereoorlog 1899-1902*". Oumam Lizzie Geldenhuys also mentions him in her "*Oorlogsherinneringe*" where the Vredefort, Kroonstad and Bothaville burgers numbered about two thousand men.

A police presence, with about 40 troopers was left behind and a Colonel Huddleston was sent as the Assistant Commissioner of Bothaville. Vels the earlier Resident Justice of the Peace of the OFS government is appointed Magistrate (or Landdrost). Secretly he 'belonged' or was still loyal to General de Wet and Bethlehem. However, amongst ourselves a great spirit prevailed to rejoin the Commando. Secret despatches are received from Klerksdorp that Burgers were being recruited.

On one Saturday evening about **20th July** our household domestics enquired whether they could go and visit. Sunday early morning our kitchen domestic brought coffee into the bedroom and informed us that the Police in Bothaville had fled during the night and that the town was 'clean'. At 10 o'clock we went over to my Father-in-law Abram for our church service. When it was over and the dinner table was being laid, two

Boers arrived, one of which I knew quite well – namely Attie Marais and the other Coetzee from the Klerksdorp Commando. They brought us up to date with the state of play in the town. After dinner they went into town to find that Magistrate Nels, the telephonist and the remaining troops had been captured.

My father-in-law and I went to the ridge overlooking the town and watched the comings and goings. Shortly afterwards a good friend of ours arrived and I used his horse to report to the Boers in the town. We are ordered that all the Boers are to meet in order to report for duty. The Burgers came round to the house with their prisoners, and departed for the River. My father-in-law, Charlie and I, each armed with a rifle and ample ammunition, preceded to the town to stand guard during the night with 20 armed men. One Boer recovers his rifle from a springhare burrow, another from a hole down at the river, and others from buried hide-a-ways. Those farmers with two rifles retained one and offered the other up for re-allocation to the needy. My Father-in-law Abram re-assumed his Veldcornet role and became our leader who would deal with Mr Huddleston.

Towards the end of **July** four spies arrived from General de Wet with the request that we farmers should join his Commando. We accompanied them to General de Wet's commando.

At Schoemansdrift about 200 'Hands Uppers' gathered around an ox-wagon on which General de Wet gave a rousing speech, reminding us that we were the same burghers that we were before now, and wished we would remain loyal till the end of the war. We stayed a couple of days until we received reports that the enemy were surrounding us, coming from the direction of Kroonstad, Vereeniging, Vrede Fort, Potchefstroom etc and that our lager at Schoemansdrift should leave post haste. Our lager was extremely large with many ox-wagons and carts. We went through the drift into the Z.A.R. (South Africa Republic), in the direction of Potchefstroom, because the forces of the enemy were too great for us. The lager travelled along the river to Venterskroon, and by the time the tail end crossed the enemy were within small arms range, with the tail-end being fired on. We managed to get away and slept that night at van Vuurenskloof. All the districts were present for a Council of War, which decided that because the larger was too large that all the ox-wagons and carts should congregate at one place and left there so as not to hamper mobility. Before the final orders were issued, the enemy started bombarding the lager with artillery / cannon fire. In the haste to escape it was everyone for himself, and as pre-arranged we all got together at Cyferfontein where our Officers issued orders that we should leave our wagons behind. We had just off-saddled, while other burghers were braai-ing meat, when we got the report to saddle up. Just then enemy cannon fire fell amongst the lager tail-enders. We took up defensive positions and brought our own cannon to bear on the enemy. Unfortunately the cannon pack-horses were fatally wounded by enemy shrapnel fire, forcing us to abandon our own cannon which duly fell into their hands. They then fired on us with our own cannon! We held our position till the early hours of the next day, when we retreated in the direction of Magaliesberg. We went over the mountain at Olifantsnek and stayed for two days. The enemy soon blocked Olifantsnek and we then retreated in the direction of Mafeking. Rustenburg is also abandoned. Our president (Steyn, OFS) departed for Machadodorp to meet up with President Kruger of Z.A.R. Our lager is split into two smaller lagers – the one with all the wagons and run-down livestock is sent to Krokedilrivier to build up their strength, while the second lager with fitter horses are dispatched to Waterberg.

Oudad Jan continues his story - -

We had a Scots car with four oxen, and we surrendered our wagon to other needier. We were allocated to the 'fat' lager to confront the enemy at Olifantsnek, while the 'lean' lager traversed the Magats Nek, to make good their escape to behind the Waterberg. The two lagers met up behind the Waterberg as arranged, but by this time our own animals were in poor condition. Food was scarce and difficult to obtain. Oxen that fainted were slaughtered. Grain for the trek-oxen was also hard to come by. Near Warmbaths, General de Wet returned to the OFS with 200 men. When the enemy heard that de Wet had returned to the Free State, they set off in pursuit, leaving the lean lager alone. Many burghers were without horses, money and no food; with life being very difficult. We who had money were better off since we could still make a plan.

We set off for Donkerspoort – a barren wasteland. After travelling non-stop on horseback for 18-hours the only living creature to cross our path was a small buck. Even water was scarce. The only human life we came across was at Crocodile River, which we came to early morning. But even there getting foodstuff was not easy. Martinus van Rooyen and I rode around all day to buy an animal, but returned empty-handed. During our search we came across an abandoned homestead – the owners having fled the scene (during earlier times the natives rebelled and just a few days beforehand had murdered three people). I noticed one very big pig in the pigsty. We had had nothing to eat the whole day, and were facing another hungry night ahead. We did notice a bee-hive near the farm homestead. As we crossed the river we spotted 8 cattle, which did not belong to the lager. One pair looked like draught oxen and the rest were young calves. I decided to steal, or rather loot one two-year old calf. About a hundred metres (tree or literally foot-steps) from the river / homestead we captured the calf and slaughtered it there. We made a fire and burnt the head, to destroy any recognisable features of its horns or ears, fearing that the beast's owner would suddenly appear. We used the calf skin to fasten a 'hold-all' or type of vat (tub) under the Scots cart, within which we placed the meat off the carcase.

At sunset I went back to the homestead to see whether I could retrieve any honey from the bee-nest. Unfortunately there was no honey, but I told Martinus about the fat pig which was still in the pigsty. By moonlight Martinus killed the pig and placed all the pork in a bag and loaded the bag onto a pack-horse. We skinned the pig at the cart, and placed the meat in the vat with the beef. We now had enough food to last until we reached home. Everyone shared the meat, and firewood was plentiful. From there we went to Bethany and came across a large African township (Kafferstad), the chief being Jacobus Magalieze near the Magaliesberg. We are friendly greeted and treated hospitably. We are given bread and coffee in his home and greeted him by hand before departing further over Olifantsnek – our journey being without mishap. Because our livestock was tired and exhausted, we went from Olifantsnek to Venterstad along Schoonspruit and onto Klerksdorp towards home.

Brief Respite

On **11 September** at 4 o'clock I arrived home. Oh! What joy is was for me to meet my dear wife. No pen is worthy to describe the event. We find everything still in good health. After a couple of days at home, more and more burgers arrived in Bothaville. C.M. Rademeyer is chosen as Captain amongst those present. One corps is formed under his leadership, and decided to protect the district until further orders are received from the General. At about beginning October, General Botha (Louis) arrived in the Onder Valsch River district with one very large Commando. Orders are received to join up with his commando, which is laagered on the farm of H. Delport near Kopje Alleen.

On about **15 October** General de Wet issued orders for the destruction of the railway line from Komatipoort to Cape Town. Under General Botha we started uprooting the rail-line from Kroonstad to Ventersburg station. We used 16 spans of oxen, and dynamite to blow up the railway lines. The rails are carted into the veld by the oxen. After destroying a section of rail we returned to where the Commando was stationed. The following day our scouts reported that an enemy lager had trekked out from Kroonstad and was headed in the direction of Bothaville. On the orders of General Botha, I was sent by ex-Commandant Nel to warn the Bothaville Landdrost to prepare them for the English column that was heading their way. I arrived at the Magistrate in the evening to deliver my instructions, and then proceeded to my own near-by home. On the **19 October** we received a report that the enemy were at Proclamation drift. My father-in-law and I herded our livestock – cattle and sheep – and took flight to the Vaal River. We only left behind a slaughter sheep and a couple of milk cows for use by our wives.

On the morning of **20 October** we had no option but to choose the "rabbit road" in order to stay out of the enemy's hands. We went to Dood's Drift on the Vaal River, leaving our wives to the mercy of the enemy.

On **23rd October** got a report from our spies that the enemy had left Bothaville and returned to Kroonstad, and with the sad news that the enemy had taken our wives away. We then returned to Bothaville and found that which can best be described as Sodom and Gomorra! Houses has been blown up with dynamite and set alight. I immediately went to my own home to find the walls all burnt down, destroyed and ruined. But above all the capture of my wife and child was the most sorrowful.

The following women were taken; my wife A.E. Geldenhuys, my mother-in-law Judith Preller, Mrs Blommestein, Mrs Rademeyer and Miss Bosman. All the women-folk and children had their houses destroyed and were accommodated in the church school buildings and in the parsonage. Some of the women were virtually naked because their clothes had been burnt.

Blowing up and burning farm houses

Before

The explosion

After

Meanwhile, de Wet's movements were as follows: General de Wet crossed the Vaal on **27th October** while being pursued by General Charles Knox and De Lisle – making good his escape during a violent thunderstorm. Knox and De Lisle headed north, but Colonel Le Gallais's mounted men headed in the opposite direction. De Wet halted near Bothaville to refit, and was caught by surprise by Major Lean with forty men of the 5th Mounted Infantry who stumbled on three weary Boers sleeping upon the veldt. Just beyond the rise was De Wet's laager – over a thousand men sleeping, horses grazing and wagons out spanned. Without a moment to lose, Lean called for reinforcements while opening fire upon the Boer camp. In an instant there was a hive of activity as De Wet rushed for their horses and made good their escape from the killing ground. Meanwhile a rearguard action that occupied an enclosed kraal and a farmhouse kept Lean at bay. This allowed the Boers to make a flanking counter-attack. By this time the reinforcements from Le Gallais had arrived on the scene, but were still outnumbered by the Boers.

The British took shelter in a small stone shed – but it was here that a Ross of the Durhams was wounded, and Colonel Le Gallais got himself killed. A Major Taylor of U gun Battery assumed command and gallantly kept up the barrage of the Boer stronghold. The battle raged on till well past eight-thirty, while several companies of Australians reinforcements also arrived. Just before the British and Australians were about to storm the farmhouse, a white flag was hoisted and 114 Boers surrendered. Nine Boers died, including Veldcornets Jan Viljoen of Heilbron and Van Zijl of the Cape Colony. Between twenty and thirty Boers were wounded that day – including the State Attorney Jacob or Japie de Villiers and Jan Rechter (also spelt Richter - the latter subsequently died as a result of his wounds). De Wet lost six Krupp field guns, a pom-pom, 20 supply wagons and 1000 head of cattle. The British lost twelve killed (including four officers, one of which was Major Welch) and thirty-three wounded. Thomas Pakenham, in his *The Boer War*, published 1979, claims that 25 Boers were killed and 130 captured, of which 30 were wounded. Surprisingly, he also quotes De Wet's *Three Years War*!

From a Boer perspective, written by Hilogarfste Piet S Lombard, in his "*Uit Die Dagboek van 'n Wildeboer*" (Out of the Diary of an Untamed Farmer), De Wets commando had trekked through Bothaville at four o'clock and found the town nearly totally burnt down by the English. They were en route to Hoopstad and arrived at Rooibult where the battle took place, where they were caught by surprise and President Steyn who had a rude awakening just managed to escape on his horse named Boetie. The Boer spies had just returned to the camp to report no danger, and while Lombard was fetching his horse, the surprise attack was sprung. The Presidents buggy, as well as his overcoat and rifle, fell to the Brits as spoils of war. In addition to the casualties already mentioned, Lombard reports that General Froneman, Komdt. Jan Theron and Tom Brain also escaped wounded. He says 120 burgers were captured by the British (Parkenham claims 130, albeit including 30 wounded).

Back to Oudad's diary:

Gert Pieterse was appointed Justice of the Peace. He had 25 men under him and received a report from General Botha to join his Commando. We then went during the night, crossing the railway line at Holfontein Siding and arrived the following day at General Botha. Gert Pieterse is instructed to operate in the old district Valsch River – returning the same day and crossing the railway line at Bosrand. Later on a report is received to join General de Wet's Commando at old Mr Muller on the Valsch River. Just as we were about to enjoy a delicious Christmas dinner, we received a report that the enemy was nearby. I and couple of others are sent out to spy when I discovered that I had lost my rifle. After spending a whole day searching I found my rifle on a path I had used earlier. We spent four nights at Mohemskuil, the farm of Jurie Steyn, then onto Renoster River. There we joined up with Captain Pieter van der Merwe's Commando. Old Year's Eve was spent on the farm of Jacobus le Roux. New Years day we were sent out to scout for a suitable rail crossing since the railway was being regularly patrolled by the enemy. New Years Eve we departed with the intent of a safe crossing. About 800 metres another pair of scouts was sent to see whether the coast was clear, but got lost and went in another direction. After a while we presumed it was safe to cross. The night was pitch-black. As we arrived at the siding the enemy spotted us and fired flares in the air. Not only did we manage to cross, Captain van der Merwe succeeded in blowing up the railway line in seven places. We also caught a native guard asleep. He is punished with 25 sjambok lashes for sleeping on duty, and sent on his way back to the siding. We off-saddled at sunrise to prepare meals. Father-in-law A. Preller, who was our chosen Veldcornet, together with Captain Pieter van der Merwe left to report to General C.R. de Wet. They returned in the afternoon and instructed us to immediately saddle up to join up with General de Wet, which we duly did just before sun-set. We then trekked back in the direction of the railway line. This large Commando consisted of 14 wagons with large spans of oxen and about 600 horsemen.

The Year 1901

About 2 o'clock in the morning **2nd January 1901** we crossed the railway near Rooiwal Siding on the Renoster (Rhino) River. No one knows where we are headed or what the aims of the Commando are. At sunrise we arrived at the farm Gansvlei. We rested all day and in the evening we received orders from the General to saddle up and returned in the direction of Rooiwal Siding. At 11 o'clock at night we arrived at the farm of General de Wet, where the empty wagons are driven to the river to uplift buried ammunitions from the earlier battle of Rooiwal. The 14 wagons are heavily laden with cannon and Lee-Metford ammunition.

We returned to the railway where we helped the ox-wagons to cross. Father-in-law Abram was appointed Veldcornet the previous day by General de Wet, and instructed to protect the Lower Valsch River district, care for the women and provisions for them. We off-saddled at Gansvlei. After a good night's rest we proceeded to our area, stopping over at the farm Leeuwkuil. There we met old widow M. Nel who had come out from Kroonstad and we were very relieved to learn that our wives and children were well. From there we went to the farm of Conrad Bezuidenhout, which became our base. J Geldenhuys is caught on suspicion and it was my turn, with Jan Neuwenhuis to escort him to Wolmaranstad Z.A.R. At that time the Transvaal Military was based at Wolmaranstad. We are granted eight days leave. I visited friends till my leave was over. When we arrived at Bothaville we heard that the Commando had been called up to the Cape Colony, and had already departed a couple of days ago. Jan Bester was appointed Veldcornet in charge of a small group of men, and we were instructed to join him. Veldcornet Bester made his base on the farm Enkeldoorn, belonging to Mr Stefanes Nel. The Veldcornet appointed me as his secretary to keep his books and draw up lists and reports which is sent monthly to the Generals. J. Hattingh is appointed General as well as relief for Chief General C.R. de Wet.

On **2nd February 1901** we went with Veldcornet Bester to Kroonstad to seize and loot. We spent the night near the home of David Malan and while it was still dark we scouted what was available. We managed to seize 7,000 sheep, 400 cattle and 70 horses. Natives that tried to escape to the town were shot. We sent the loot on with 8 men and a few natives, with the remaining 30 men split ahead and behind to guard the loot. At sunrise the tail end was still within cannon fire range. Despite the enemy opening fire on us, nobody was injured. I was lucky to disarm one Khaki. The horse saddle and bridle was gifted to me by the Veldcornet. Each burgher was permitted to choose one cow and 15 sheep. However, my heart was heavy knowing that my wife and family were in the town and that I could not even see them.

A short while after the looting, Commandant Theron arrived from the other side of the rail to act over us. At the council of war it is decided to establish a special constabulary, and under the direction of V.C Joseph van Biljon I together with two other burgers were appointed policemen. The instructions I got from the Commandant was to take charge of the staffing of Government buildings and to ensure non-essential personnel together with persons staying at home after their leave had expired are commandeered to serve with the Commandos. The area of responsibility stretched between the Valsch and Renoster Rivers. I made my base in the middle of the area, at Verdwaalpan, the farm of J. Engelbreg, which had good stables for our horses. I was supported by the Commandant to requisition feed for the horses on O.V.S. Government expense, and which I made very good use of. I had five horses at my disposal. During the month of **July 1901**I received instructions to get all the burgers that were at their homes were required to assemble on the farm of Markus Willeman, at which a council of war was held. The decision taken was for all active service burgers to immediately join their Commandos. Burger Isaac Goosen was ordered to join the Commando but refused to do so. He declined to take up arms but volunteered to assist in any other capacity. Commandant Theron became impatient and sent a report to the Chief Commandant who replied a week later that Burger Goosen be placed “across the line” (to be handed over to the English?). Unfortunately it befell me to take him across the line. The Commandant issued me with a written order. I duly went to him and informed him of my unpleasant task that I was to take him prisoner in order to take him across the line. I had a miserable scene with his mother and sister and leave them behind without any care. I explained my innocence in the matter to the mother and sister, stating that if I failed in my unpleasant duty that I would find myself in exactly the same predicament. I took him to the Middelspruit farm of H.J. Geldenhuys (an Uncle – Hendrik Jacobus?) from where he was on his own. I left him with my best wishes, knowing my own circumstances concerning my dear wife.

My father-in-law and I were very lucky with our sheep, but during the month of **August 1901**, 15 enemy lagers went around our district to round up and slaughtered more than 2000 sheep and left them in a heap. It was pitiful to see the sights and cruel manner in which the sheep were killed. We still had our cattle, between 2 and 300. Jan Bester resigned as Veldcornet and Hermanus Kritzinger was chosen as the replacement Veldcornet. Commandant Theron and Veldcornet J. van Biljon made a voluntary chorus (Koor) to go to the Cape Colony. Instead of Commandant Theron, Jan Nagel is sent across the spoor. However, a large number of Lower Valsch River district burgers were dissatisfied with Commandant Jan Nagel. They wanted Kritzinger in his stead. Brother-in-law Charlie Preller also went to the Cape Colony with instructions and joined Chief Commandant Kritzinger. The police received call-up from Komdt Nagel to join his Commando as before (previously). In my time I was with my Commando V.C. Kritzinger took me on as his secretary like previously. V.C Kritzinger was the relief during the absence of Komdt Nagel. I was thus simultaneously adjutant to Veldcornet Kritzinger as well as doing sentry (Brand wag) duty. I endured one dreadful night with the wind blowing so strong that men could hardly remain upright, as well as cold. In the morning we returned to our base. Because I had slept so little the night before, I took the opportunity to catch up with some sleep. While I was asleep, my Father-in-law Abram came in to wake me up (he used to be the Bothaville magistrates clerk), and to my big surprise my brother-in-law Charlie was with him. There was much gladness to meet him after an absence of six months during which nothing had been heard of him. We had even heard that he had been captured, and even killed – and what joy to meet him now in person. My father-in-law had planned to return in the afternoon, but I persuaded him to stay over. About 3 o'clock in the afternoon a sentry came rushing in – his horse was drenched with sweat. While anxiously waiting for him to catch his breath, thinking that the enemy may be close at hand, he blurted out that one lady had come out from the Kroonstad and he wanted to consult with the Veldcornet as what to do about it. While this was going on I was within earshot. The sentry said that the woman was Jan's mother, and she wished to see him. Oh, what great news that was. My brother-in-law Charlie and I immediately mounted our horses and raced off to meet her near Driekopjes.

My pen is not worthy to write of the joy and gladness of our meeting. We hugged each other and it took awhile before we could utter a word. Before long my mother informed me that my wife was still well, but also the heartbroken news that my darling daughter had died on 15th August 1901. No one is able to commiserate my grief at the bitter news. My mother took a photo from her bag, which showed her corpse, which left a scar on my heart. We had been separated for eleven months but it was good to see that she was still healthy and good in spirit. My mother also informed me that my father had been seriously ill with pneumonia, but was fully recovered. We then went to the farm of Widow M. Nel under orders of Veldcornet Kritzinger. After a period of rest I received further instructions to go to Doorndraai. At that time ex-V.C. Bester had his family at Doorndraai.

There Father-in-law Abram heard the glad tidings that ma-Preller and the children were in good health, and that my wife with Ma-Preller had the same day gone to apply for the permit to come out of the concentration camp. The reason for the 'pass' was because of a British authority Proclamation that those burgers who had not handed over their weapons by **15 September 1901** (Readers are reminded, that at about this time, on 7th September 1901, Commandant Robert Clunie (Robbie) Preller was wounded in the Colesberg region. He was captured and sent to the prisoner of war camp Shajahanpur in India) would be banned for life from South Africa. Our women had given the excuse to convey the proclamation to their husbands and try to convince them to hand over their weapons. However, my mother was a loyal Afrikaner and advised me that instead of handing my weapons over that I should instead hold out to the bitter end. Two days after my mother had come out; I met my dear wife in an indescribable meeting. It was with deep grieving over the loss of our baby, but we clung and hugged one another. The experience of our loss made a deep impression on her. My father-in-law left Charlie behind while he took ma-Preller to Bothaville, despite her coming out from Kroonstad. I decided to remain at J. Bester until such time that my mother was obliged to return to Kroonstad. When my mother returned to Kroonstad, I took my wife to Bothaville and we decided that she would not return. I still had my car and horses, and she would escape in the event of the enemy appearing. She would be cared for by her father whenever I would be on commando. At that time fairly large female lagers were quite popular, who would tail the men, because to remain in their homes resulted in them being caught by the enemy.

On **1st October 1901** we took flight because an enemy lager arrived in Bothaville. We travelled in the direction of Zandspruit, taking our cattle with us. On the 2nd October before sunrise the enemy had caught up with us. We were forced to abandon our cattle and only those women who had cars were able to escape the enemy. Those without were taken prisoner. After the enemy had withdrawn between Kroonstad and Ventersburg were we able to return to our home district. I took my wife to the Coffeefontein farm of van Biljon because it was unsafe to remain in Bothaville. The enemy were building block houses from Kroonstad along the Valsch River towards Bothaville.

We were invited by my Father-in-law Abram to spend Christmas with them at Balkfontein, the farm of Louw Greyling. The day before we took all our shackles ("zak en pak ") with us, because it was unwise to leave anything behind as should the enemy appear unexpectedly, ones possessions would all be lost. Christmas morning the meal is prepared and rusks are baked. While the food was still on the stove we received a report that the enemy was at Bothaville, about forty-minutes by horse-back from Balkfontein. Everything was then "rep en roer" - confusion and bustle – horses are fetched, food is stashed, and within an hour we were on our way. Our Christmas dinner came to nought as the food had not yet cooked properly.

On the **26th December 1901** we heard that the enemy had gone back to Koolmyndrift (Coal-mine-drift), where they were making another block-house line along the Vaal River. We returned to Coffeefontein. Father Preller promised to spend New Year's Day with us. Old Year's Eve father arrived with all the cattle, trek, etc. We made ourselves ready to spend this day together, seeing that Christmas day was such a large disappointment.

The Year 1902

On New Year's morning, Charlie and Johnnie Odendaal left with my buggy (car) to look for and fetch potatoes and fruit on the farm of C. Cloete. We slaughtered one fat sheep. At about 8 o'clock in the morning we heard cannon-fire coming from the direction of Bothaville. The order was immediate flight. I went to round up the cattle, but found that the enemy had already impounded them. I hastened back to father-Preller to tell him that the enemy were five minutes away and no time can be wasted. What was I to do, seeing that Charlie had taken my buggy? My wife had no option to take all her things and climb up on her father's car, and luckily managed to get away. All the calves had been left in the cattle-kraal. During the night most of the cows returned to the kraal where the calves were. We also managed to round up a few stray cattle. However, the enemy was in possession of the few cattle I had originally sought, and they being herded to Driekopjes, while we headed back to Coffeefontein. At that time the Block-houses were right across Besterkraal. A Council of War was held and the decision taken that one of the women lagers should scale down and trek to Boshof. We were also later obliged to seek safety because the block-houses were getting closer and closer to Coffeefontein. We left just in time for Coffeefontein near Eskol, the home of P. van Biljon.

On about **5th February 1902** we went with a commando of 200 men led by Commandant van Bergen of Hoopstad to look for opportunities to attack the Block-houses. We aimed at starting from Kroonstad, and took up position amongst the ruins (walls) of the farm Strydfontein of elderly David Malan. A pair of armed native "scouts" was caught by the burgers and in terms of the O.F.S. Government Proclamation, they were duly shot. We then went along the line of Block-houses but did not find an ideal opportunity to attack any. On the farm of old Mr Piet Smit we fired on one block-house but were soon forced to retreat. Assistant Veldcornet Johannes Nel's horse was wounded slightly in the neck. We then stationed on the farm of C. Botha. District Hoopstad Veldcornet Kritzinger granted me leave of absence to return to my home seeing that the Block-houses had reached Tweefontein, necessitating further relocation. I went from Eskol to the farm Modderfontein belonging to F. Pieterse. I was only there a couple of days when the order was given for the larger to trek to Boshof as per council of war determination. Father Preller and I found ourselves in the middle, not knowing what to do, whether to go with the larger or not. Eventually we arrived at the conclusion not to join the lager, because it was already large and the enemy would take great pains to lay its hands on it. We thus left the lager and made our base on the farm of van Rensburg – with the thought that the enemy would not hinder us there. The nearest enemy was then at Bothaville, about five-hours by horse-back to van Rensburg.

On the **19th February 1902** we took the decision that the women-folk would no longer try to escape the clutches of the enemy, because very few safe havens remained for them. We then decided to hide their cars / buggies in the banks of the Vaal River, so as not to fall into enemy hands in the event of capture. We would then stay with them by day, but would sleep with our horses in the veld by night. On the 19th February we despatched two buggies to fetch mielies from Eskol so that we would have enough provisions to store up. The buggies returned late that night. We enquired whether any sign of the enemy was seen – and the reply was that everything was peaceful and quiet. The report was that the Block-houses from Kroonstad and the other from Koolmyndrift at Bothaville had been completed or unified, and there was no movement as to leaving the Block-houses. Early the morning father-Preller left to carry out reconnaissance / spying.

Captured

Thursday **20th February 1902** at 7 o'clock p.m. was the appointed time that we also fell into the hands of our arch enemy, and what bitter moments we endured to be separated from our dearly beloved, not knowing whether we would once again set eyes upon each other on this world. Within the hour we left van Rensburg, district Hoopstad. That is the place our bitter cup was emptied. We were taken in the direction of Commando Drift, and after about an hour the officer ordered us to out-span till late afternoon. It was extremely hot in the blazing sun, while we encamped next to a large rock. A goat-ewe was slaughtered, which we then had to cook as our meals for the whole day. The native troops meanwhile rounded up sheep into a kraal and then commenced killing them. I witnessed with my own eyes the senseless maiming and slaughter of innocent animals. A half wagon axle was used to batter the heads of the sheep, while others had their throats slit and left to bleed to death. The poor animals would wobble and lurch till the loss of blood resulted in a painful death. By night fall I was placed in a pigsty and told to make our beds there. About an hour after going to bed, the enemy fired two rockets into the night sky. It gave us quite a fright, while at the same time we heard gun-fire coming from the direction of Bothaville. Like me, most of the prisoners had little sleep that night.

On **21st February** we arrived just outside Bothaville, at Valsch River Drift. We were ordered to get off the wagons, and told to strip down; in like manner which the Boers did to any British captures (Uitskud!). We were then ordered to take off our trousers. I was then asked by the officer whether we used to take the shoes from British soldiers, to which I replied in the affirmative whenever the shoes were in better condition than our own. No sooner having said that, I was ordered to take my own shoes off. This I did as an Afrikaner. We were then marched, barefoot and without trousers, from outside the town to the Magistrates Office, which served as the Boer Prisoner camp. We were detained in Bothaville for five days. Father and Uncle Michael were taken from us and placed in goal. Our food was raw lamb, and J van den Berg and I were detailed to go and cook it. We welcomed the task as it afforded us the opportunity to get some fresh air. We are continuously questioned on our knowledge of British columns, with Sergeant Jones placed to take charge of us, and we duly acknowledge the good treatment and care we got from him. We were searched thoroughly, not only our pockets but had to strip naked while every hem and fold of our pants, shirts and jackets were gone over. Thank God nothing incriminating was found.

On **27th February** at 2 o'clock in the morning we left Bothaville in mule wagons for Kroonstad. After a two-hour (horse-back) journey we arrived at Rustrant. From there we were placed 20 people on one mule-wagon drawn by six trek-oxen to Driekopjes where we were met friendly by Major Porter, the English officer. He placed us in one large Hospital tent, gave us enough food and also tobacco.

28th February early morning we left Driekopjes, for Kroonstad, with wagons drawn by mules. The wagon I was on was in-spanned with 10 dark brown yellow-mouth mules. I must admit that I have never been behind a span of horses that were as good as this span of mules. At about 9 o'clock we arrived at Kroonstad station. We were off-loaded and then marched to the old Government School which the enemy had converted to one large goal. While walking through the town we met many friends, many gazing at us with sad eyes, while many others were clothed in sheep-skins on the outside and woollen inside. We were hospitably received my family and friends who gave us cake, coffee, fruit, clothing etc. We were supplied with so many goods that the no (government) rations were issued us. We were, however, forbidden to speak to anybody. Luckily, two Corporals did allow me to catch sight of my sisters Bettie, Maria and my young brother Hendry – and with relief I heard that my father (HJ Geldenhuys) and my brother had been sent to Durban to board a ship.

This was another bitter cup to empty. I saw my dear mother six paces from me. I was given the privilege to speak one word with one another. Oh! What sadness to see her being led away with tears in her eyes, by a guard despite her having tried by all means to bid farewell to her son, not knowing when next the opportunity may arise on this earth. But one thing I know – God never sleeps. Such cruel behaviour is also written up in His book. Our jail is a wretched place. 52 prisoners are placed in a cell, infested with lice that roamed everywhere like ants. We spent our time killing as many lice as we could. My father, Uncle Michael and R. Frank Brewis were placed in another room (cell) where they are slightly better off. Church services are held regularly amongst us, by my old friend Ernst van Biljon. We were summoned in lots of 10 to report to the Intelligence Officer. I was accused of misbehaviour of taking a certain Bastiaan Crouse prisoner, and tying him up with a hide chain, and had threatened him that he would be shot. This I admitted to, having acted under the orders of Veldcornet Bester. The reason being that he had previously escaped custody. In front of the office stood many astonished acquaintances. That they were still well clothed the acquaintances were under British protection as Hands Uppers gave shortened versions. I was then escorted by armed guard back to the prison.

The **5th March 1902** was my mothers' birthday. It was heart-breaking that I was so close to her but prohibited from wishing her well with her birthday. During the evening of the 4th I was visited by my in-law family, family Rademeyer and sister Bettie where they had received a Pass from the Provost Marshal – and it was one joyful meeting. E van Biljon, M van Biljon, Gert van der Merwe and I were called over to where my father and Uncle Michael were for the meeting – with one crying and the other laughing for joy! With sunset quite a few other friendly women also came to visit. It was one huge friendly meeting, which went on throughout the night. In the evening we held a Church service to thank God for our blessings. That same night we were told that we would leave for Bloemfontein in the morning.

I need to mention a couple of things about Kroonstad, - I was born about 2 hours by horse-back from the town; I was christened in the town and also became a church member. My marriage was in the district Kroonstad (actually De Bank, Bothaville). We lived 4 hours by horse-back from the town, and we would come in for shopping two or three times every month. No-one hassled me and I was free to come and go as I wished. Now I was held under armed guard, by bayonet, and no longer had the freedom to go alone to the town-house that we had. On the 5th March at 8 o'clock we bid a heart-wrenching farewell to family and friends, with Godspeed and the parting message to remain loyal and hold out to the bitter end. We were lined up four-abreast and marched to the railway station under armed escort. At the station we were placed in one open, dirty coal-truck, where we had to endure the blazing sun all day. We left with sun-set, travelling past the Women's (Refugee) Prisoners camp, where they waved white handkerchiefs in a farewell salute. Having been in the blazing sun all day, we stopped at Smaldeel station for the night.

On the morning **6th March** we travelled another very hot day on the Krolen (Boeren), arriving Bloemfontein about midday, and placed behind wooden bars – spending another bitter hot day in the sun. We were marched to the Town Hall and onto the

Prisoners Camp. There we were met by more of our friends amongst which was Commandant Rabie who told us that they were treated fairly. We had no complaints about the food, and that evening E. van Biljon and I were treated to a pleasant bath. While I had the opportunity I also washed my shirt and under-pants. This P.O.W. – Prisoner of War camp at Bloemfontein measured 95 by 95 paces and held 160 men. We liked the place to a Zoo, just as crowded as Kroonstad as well as the train. The other Boers told us that every Saturday a bunch is sent off. After 5 days on Saturday morning we were lined up in one row for Roll Call so that we could be counted. Then the Sgt produced a list and read out our names. At 4 o'clock we left for the station. There we were placed 15 Boere with a guard of 5 troopers in one horse-carriage. The truck was also cramped and we were ordered to sit-down as nobody was allowed to stand. The Lieutenant placed in charge of us was a certain __ who I will never forget. It resulted in the rough and cruel behaviour metered out to us.

We spent till **9th March 1902** there, our friends on the train being E van Biljon, Gert van der Merwe, Jonathan van Schalkwyk, EJ Holtzhuizen, J Rabie, NS Realer, my father-in-law Abram Preller and I. We eventually arrived at Kroonstad and spent the night on the train because the enemy was scared to travel further at night with the POW train. That was the morning of 10th March. One of the sentries guarding us said that a number of Boere had crossed the railway line the night before. Another complaint that I had taken note of was the fact that the natives were permitted to mock and tempted us without hindrance. Their day of judgement will one day arrive. The day thereafter we arrived at Elandsfontein. There we met other captures from the local area, amongst which was Old Oud Bekket.

We stayed awhile and left in the morning of **11 March**. From there we travelled over Heidelberg and in the evening arrived at Charlestown. We nearly died of starvation, not having had anything to eat since leaving Bloemfontein. The following morning a certain Mr Thom and my Father-in-law Abram wrote a letter of complaint addressed to the Officer in charge Charlestown whether it was their custom not to feed their prisoners and further brought the humanitarian provisions of the Geneva and Haag Conventions to their attention. That solved the problem in that we were then provided with food and tea. We continued our journey, travelling past Colley se Kop (Amajuba) where we observed many attractive Punten. That evening we arrived at Ladysmith. We saw many battlefields along the line of rail where the enemy had got a hiding. We did not see much of Ladysmith because it was dark by the time we got there.

Then on the morning of the **13th March** we left Ladysmith and saw lovely plantations and beautiful mountains (Drakensberg). We crossed the Tugela River and saw thousands of British graves. Oud Bekket explained all the battlefields in which he also fought, and pointed out the banana and pineapple plantations en route. At about 11 o'clock we could see the sea for the first time, way over to the east. It looked like one very large cloud. Some could not believe it, but were convinced the closer we came. About 12 o'clock we arrived in Durban. Durban is one very large town. The night before we had stayed over at Pieter Maritz burg (Pietermaritzburg) where the guard prohibited us from sitting down and continuously shouted at us to sit down. I retorted that did he want to push us through the floor of the iron coal-truck.

Shipped to India

At Durban there was a small Tug that shuttled to and fro to a large ship, the Aurania, about two miles (3km) out to sea. A big crowd of people came to stare curiously at us Boers. As we neared the Tug, we were photographed about a dozen times. Eventually we turned our backs to the photographer so that he had to be satisfied with whatever (photographs) was already taken. The sea was very rough on the 2 mile trip and quite a few of the men were dreadfully sea-sick, which was a sorry sight to see. They wretched all over the place, amongst which was poor Uncle Willem Meintjies. We sailed to the Aurania where the Tug was tied to the bigger ship, and a huge basket lowered to hoist prisoners and troops up. The basket held 7 to 8 persons, who were hoisted 15 feet (nearly tree metres) to the upper deck. On deck we met other friends like Dirk Jordaan and Ferdinand Preller, the father of Gustav Preller, and others as well. To my disappointment, I had hoped to find my father and brother Pieter, but learnt that they had already departed for the strange and far-off country India. It is nearly impossible for me to write anything about this large vessel. We were placed in hold 2 Travel 9. Frank Brewis was made Corporal over us, and in the hold everyone sweated profusely. In every doorway and passage was a Tommy, fearing that we would jump overboard into the sea. A lot of fish swam around the ship, which we marvelled at. It was a pitiful sight to see how forlorn a lot of Boers had resigned themselves to. For three days I wanted nothing to do with food due to an upset tummy. However, after the three days, everything was right with me. Everybody was issued with one hammock and a blanket. Beneath deck there were a lot of hooks to hang the hammocks in which we slept. We could see that the ship was preparing to sail because a lot of meat, cabbage and potatoes, etc. was taken onboard.

Wednesday evening **19th March 1902** at 7 o'clock we departed Durban for the so-called Bombay. Thursday morning 20th March 1902 when we got on deck we saw nothing else but only blue skies, sea waves and no land in sight at all. We saw flying fish for the first time – they looked like small birds jumping out of the sea. After breakfast we were required to scrub the decks, tables, knives and forks. I was made Corporal in charge of six men to scrub the floors. At 10 o'clock inspection is held by the Ships Officer, and our team is given credit for the best job done on the ship. As the weather deteriorated the first couple of days, more and more people became sea-sick, while many other Boere were bewildered with everything. About 15 paces from the ship we could see fish the size of a pig that would hop on the surface like a springhare does on the ground. Two of our burgers die on board and what a dreadful sight to see them buried at sea, their bodies dumped overboard to be eaten by game fish (sharks?). Regular Church services are held onboard, with prayers to see mother earth again. After 14 days having left Durban, landfall resembling a large mist-belt was sighted. Oh! What glad tidings amongst everyone.

Whist still far out to sea we were met by small boats. After having sighted land it took another three hours to get to Bombay. The anchor is lowered at about one mile (1½ km) out to sea and that evening a notice is pinned to a door to say that the ship was under guarantee. Oh what a setback! Everyone expected that we would need to remain there for a month! Two Men of War ships with searchlights arrived in the evening to guard us during the night. We were kept on board ship, at anchor in Bombay, from Wednesday afternoon till Friday 2 p.m., when we boarded a train to Umballa. We are placed six persons to a third class compartment – the most comfortable ride since our capture. We travelled from Bombay to a railway station, whose name escapes me, where we stayed overnight in a very large barracks. Towards late afternoon we departed by train again – and have the opportunity to observe the country India. We see thousands of Indians (Coolies, spelt Koellies, in high Dutch.) going about their business – as far as the eye can see. Cattle are seen initially in small herds but latter larger herds are noted. Buffalo are more plentiful, very docile by nature, but quite useless as my father would say. Goats and horses appear identical to those found in South Africa. Cattle however have a different shape and are rather smaller than in S.A. I saw one poor creature laden with 60 bundles of hay and with the Coolie riding on top – so heavily laden that one had difficulty in recognising what sort of animal it was. India does not appear to have any wagons, only cars that are drawn by two oxen or buffaloes, and then without a Jukskei.

South African / American wagons would have up to sixteen or eighteen spans of oxen. 'Cars' or buggies would invariably be horse drawn, and thus differed from Indian wagons.

A rope is fastened around the ox's neck which is then hitched to the Scots cart and which would be laden with goods for transport. I saw one cart laden with just as much hay that would be loaded or carried by one S.A. ox wagon! Sheep in India are similar to the black cross-breed woollen Marino sheep as found in S.A. We also saw springbucks as if they originated from SA, except that the brown stripe is not as bright or broad as in S.A. The Indian cart has broader wheel rims, without tyres, and the oxen are harnessed as what our horse carriages would be in SA. The coolie sits on the drawbar between the two oxen and prods them with a short staff about 60cm (two and a half feet) long. Some even have a sharp pen or nail shaped point with which to prod the poor animal. I am of the opinion that the law regarding cruelty to animals is nonexistent or practiced in India. I witnessed some oxen with raw, open wounds caused by mishandling or ill-fitting harnesses. The donkeys here are the same as ours. The poor dumb animal is so heavily laden with bricks, sand and stone etc. that the animals sometimes collapse. The pigs are so scrawny that the wind can topple them over. Indians tend to live on hilltops in straw-huts similar to the poor blacks in SA. Land preparation and ploughing is done with two oxen drawing a wooden plough. The topsoil is tilled for only about 1½ inches deep, because of the scarcity of water here. Wells are seen everywhere with Indians using what seems to be wooden gears to draw or 'pump' water in clay pots to the fields – usually with the use of two ox drawn carts. Hilltops also had many monuments that had been build many hundreds of years ago, to which pilgrim Indians would visit. We passed the Holy City in the distance, at which many Indians were present.

Our second stopover since leaving Bombay was Jhansi. We were accommodated in a very large Marque tent and served with sheep meat and a rice soup in which there were quite a few flies – so much so that some of us could not stomach the meal. We were soon surrounded by Indians that streamed in from the east and west to barter for old clothing etc. We even experienced theft, this one robbed of his jacket, while the next lost a blanket. Each prisoner was issued with one small canteen from which to eat or drink. We departed from there at about 3 o'clock, travelling overnight till the next afternoon without getting any food, only water until we arrived at Umballa on the 7 April 1902. We had been travelling for a month and many were relieved to arrive at our destination after so many discomforts and deprivations.

Umballa Prisoner of War camp

Umballa is the Prisoner of War camp at which we were stationed. We were escorted from the railway station by four heavily armed guards marching in front, and four at the rear. Each POW carrying his small bundle of possessions on his back. At the camp we were pleased to meet up with many acquaintances like B.J.V. de Klerk, J. Venter, and G. Coetzee on the southern side, everyone anxious of any news regarding their families and wellbeing in South Africa. I was fortunately in the position to inform them that it was still well with them. I also enquired whether anyone knew of the whereabouts of my father and brother Pieter and whether they were at this camp, but nobody could shed any light on the mystery.

We were placed under Corporal Heckrood in Sector 2 tent 14. Then we got our first meal of bread and rice. I t was not of the best but because of our hunger we found it very tasty. We soon befriended everyone – in our tent we had my father-in-law

Abram Preller from De Bank, Kroonstad, myself Jan Geldenhuys De Bank Kroonstad, Ernst van Biljon Bothaville Kroonstad, Gert van der Merwe Bothaville Kroonstad, Jonathan van Schalkwyk Waaifontein Philippolis, Johannes Rabie, Woest Arabia Fauresmith, William L. Realier dorp Thaba Nchu and E.J. Holtzhuizen junior Glen Liding O.F.S. Every occupant was worthy of the title of True Afrikaner – all living in a tent measuring some 18 feet wide by 22 feet long. The plot on which the tent stood measured 50 feet square and the size of the camp was 400 yards square, with 23 strands of wire encircling the camp with one security guard outside the fence. At night the perimeter was lit up with electric lights with a roll call held at nine o'clock when everyone in the tent is required to line up outside and then a cannon shell is fired for lights-out. In the morning's roll call is held at half past six and all our furniture consisting of eight bamboo beds 6 feet long by 2 feet 6 inches wide, each person having two bed sheets, one blanket, spread, and one coir pillow with pillow-case. 4 Kist's for every two men, one Kist, 2 benches, 1 table, 8 plates, knives, forks, spoons and mugs - - every morning our food is dished up; 8 loaves of bread, coffee, tea and sugar and during the week beef, rice and potatoes. On Sundays we get lambs meat meal-soup, and potato. We have a normal round basin and each person is required to fill it with water for his own use. It the afternoons when it is a bit cooler the men usually participate in football and cricket – about half the camp is involved with all sorts of games and religious services are regularly attended. There are quite a few elephants in the camp at Umballa, and they are used to carry allsorts on their backs as would also be carried by carts and wagons.

At midday a canon is fired to signal 12 o'clock and to summon the Boers to fetch their food rations. Two tent occupants work a nightly shift and are required to keep watch, sweep out the tent, make coffee and fetch water. For a slice of bread one is able to hire a Coolie to do the washing-up – which is sufficient to gratify the Coolie. Hawks and predator birds as found in S.A. are numerous and very tame here. They have the habit of swooping down onto the food basins to snatch pieces of meat whenever the basins of food rations are collected from the kitchen (cook-house). Our names are called to collect clothing and shoes.

I need to record in this diary my sorrow over the unholy practices on Sundays. I was of the view that the Sabbath was also respected by the English government, but even Christians ignored carried on with their daily chores, making bricks, carting sand, building barracks and houses, ploughing fields and operating trains, etc..

We were informed of the heat, and also experienced that in the beginning of summer it would be as hot as the hottest day in the middle of summer in S.A. Several articles are extremely cheap here, like cigars are purchased 1/- one shilling per one hundred. Other goods are priced the same as in S.A. or even more expensive. Everyone wears cork helmets and hats because of the blazing sun – with some suffering sun-stroke.

Tuesday morning **8th April** we are taken to have our names, ages, homes, farms and districts recorded, and then returned to the Camp. I also took advantage of writing a letter to my sister Bettie and expressed our longing for our beloved fatherland South Africa.

Thursday 10th April I again went out 'on orders' to the barracks and to see who would accept parole. Unfortunately John Rabie was cornered and my Father-in-law Abram petitions the older folk to relocate to the cooler mountainous camp. However, my father-in-law pleaded to rather stay behind at Umballa to be amongst his friends. His request was granted. John Rabie then changed his mind and went back to ask to stay put, his request was similarly granted. Thereupon the officer retorted "You'll sweat for it", and he then returned to the Camp. That evening we are told that we go on a route march in the morning. In the afternoon, to my amazement I saw the work that many Boers had made – watch chains, breast brooches, tie-rings and other rings, made from wooden pipes, breastpin studs, walking sticks, cigar holders etc. masterpieces beautifully made.

Friday 11th April at six o'clock we went on our route march of about 3 miles. I found the outing very pleasant just to get out doing the walk. I bought a hand operated machine to learn all about making neck-ties – in order to shorten the boredom in the mornings. I also received news today that there was a skirmish at the Trichenopoly POW camp in which two Boers were killed and two wounded.

Saturday 12th April it was our turn to receive our food ration. We bought pancakes at three for a penny. Ernst van Biljon conducted our evening service, taking the lesson from Genesis Chapter 12. Holtzhuizen with the nickname Tiedeldiers and I took turns to serve in front of the tent.

Sunday 13th April is the holy day celebrated by the Afrikaners in conducting religious services and the singing of psalms, hymns and other Christian hymnals. But what is happening on the other side? A large brick building is being built with no differentiation being made between a Sunday and a Monday. Coolies are doing the bricklaying, plastering, carting sand and stone with elephants etc – all happening under Christian British BEVOLKING. The general service is carried out by Captain Bosch, who came from Egypt.

Monday 14th April at half past six we again went out on a route march to a point about a mile and a half from the Camp.

Tuesday 15th April I went to the laundry to wash my longs. During the morning we heard approx 25 canon shells being fired, not very far from our Camp. We were also inspected by the Doctor, everyone lining up in single file while the doctor carried out his rounds at about four feet from us. Vader Abram Preller, Ernst van Biljon and I enjoyed a good bath before the evening sermon held by Captain Bosch. We sang Psalm 68 verse 6, Psalm 25 verse 8 and with the reading taken from Exodus 5. Our closing hymn was the last verse of our Evening song “O Vader dat U Liefd ons Nader”. When we got back from the Church Service we heard that back home Peace Talks were being held – and possibly explained while all those canon shells were fired off in the morning. We had a relatively quiet evening, because our habit was an evening prayer or “home group” meeting in the tent, lead by E. van Biljon, followed in the morning with a session led by my father-in-law Abram Preller.

Wednesday 16th April, just before midday, it became very windy resulting in a lot of dust everywhere. We heard the sad news that one of our burgers had passed away and the funeral was held at half past four in the afternoon. I did not attend the funeral but was told that the coffin / body were carried on a canon drawn by six horses and that the funeral service was conducted by the British pastor. Our evening meal was a very tasty Irish stew, with beef, potatoes and curry – the curry we cooked ourselves, having obtained it for one quarter-anna –

equivalent to one halfpenny. Gert van der Merwe and another burger prepared the meal for us. We enjoyed one lovely afternoon, calm and cool. I attended the general Worship conducted by Mr. Ebertson who pastured and took the reading from John, 15th chapter, from verse 5. We had Holy Communion and sang Psalm 146 verse 3 – holy is he, the story of Jacob and how God came to his rescue. Stories circulated in the camp that peace had been concluded with President Steyn, Generals de Wet, Botha and de le Rey and Judge Hertzog with burgers from Klerksdorp who trekked to Pretoria – and who all had dinner in Potchefstroom. We ask God to reveal the truth having also heard that agreement had been reached:-

1. All prisoners to be repatriated immediately.
2. Rebuilding all the houses destroyed and burnt by the British.
3. Every Boer farmer given a herd of sheep to commence faming again.

The prayer meeting was concluded with reading the first four verses from Corinthians 1.

Thursday 17th April was a reasonably quiet day, quite hot but nothing noteworthy happening. We had one pleasant dinner, with Tiedeldiers and I doing routine duty outside the tent. Our meal was beef with potato meal and potato soup with onions. Captain Boshof appointed me as the assistant Teacher for the youth. Prayers are held that the truth will prevail, and to give us the strength to fight the good fight. Peace news is that our leaders are still in Pretoria, engaged in negotiations. Because Ernst van Biljon was not feeling well, J. Rabie held the home-group meeting.

Friday 18th April. The British held a parade with rifles and cannons, and fired off 25 cannon shells. This made a lasting impression on me. I also received two letters – one from J. Meintjies and the other from B. Combrink – keeping us abreast of family news in S.A.

Saturday 19th April. The day is quiet. Gert van der Merwe returned today from the hospital, having reported sick yesterday. I spent the day replying to the letters I received yesterday – writing to Meintjies and B. Combrink and enquiring if they had any news of my father and brother Pieter. In the afternoon I went to watch the cricketers and football players. We also had our washing done by an Indian, on Government account. I also repaired a pair of slops, which made me think of my dear wife back home who would normally care for me. Peace talks are still doing the rounds in the camp. Our officers W. Rheeder and E. van Biljon are sickly and we hope for speedy recoveries.

Sunday 20th April. The bugle sounded the roll-call, which was the start of another pleasant Sabbath day. The eservice opened with the singing of Gesang 84 verse 8 and Gesang 58 verse 7. The reading was taken from the New Testament Acts 27 and from the Old Testament Josiah 52, and Gesang 62 verse 9. J. Rabie said the final prayer and the service ended with singing Psalm 134 verse 3. The rest of the day was spent sleeping or reading of Christian booklets. In the evening we had a prayer meeting, praying for the women and children in S.A. and those who were forced into Concentration Camps. The prayer session was opened by reading Psalm 74 – and to one's own wonderment I should mention that the Indians did not go about their normal work routines, and no one amongst us could offer an explanation.

Monday 21st April. Nothing significant happened during the day. I started making one neck-tie when my Father-in-law Abram kept me busy the whole day. Then at about one o'clock there were 62 canon shells fired off – the meaning of which we would only find out later on.

Tuesday 22nd April. The enemy fired one canon in the morning. The display occurred so close that one could see the canon firing a total of 141 times – which made us cast our minds to our beloved fatherland South Africa, where I on more than one occasion happen to be on the receiving end! I recovered a letter addressed to my father – and opened it to see what was written. It was sent by Cousin A. van der Linde. I was relieved to read, and pleased, that our family in Kroonstad was still okay. I added a couple of lines at the end of the letter and re-addressed it to father and brother Pieter at Trichenopoly camp further inland. Peace talks are doing the rounds in our camp.

Wednesday 24th April. The day was unpleasant, with the howling and dust clouds so thick that the air virtually chocked us. It was my turn to care for the tent but had difficulty in washing the dishes in the wind and all that dust. Because the teacher was sick I had to stand in for him.

Friday 25th April. We went out on a pleasant route march in the morning. We also had the doctor's inspection. Peace talk rumours are still doing the rounds in the camp.

Sunday 27th April. A quiet day – the church service is carried out by E. van Biljon. The local Indians ignored the Sabbath and continued with building of the barracks. It was Rheeler's turn to carry out Tent Duty. While going to the cookhouse to fetch our dinner, about five paces from the cookhouse, a hawk swooped down and pinched a piece of beef out of the food basin. He was compelled to return to the camp in order to cover the basin as protection from the hawks. Rumours of the peace talks seem to quieten down. The general *evening service is conducted by Captain Bosch*, with praise singing from Psalm 84 verses 1 to 6, Psalm 89.7 and the reading taken from Corinthians 5, with the last three verses being emphasised and ending with singing a Psalm.

Tuesday 29th April. It is my tour of duty in front of the Tent. The day was calm and hot. I made application to have ourselves photographed and was granted a pass from 3 to 6 o'clock – to leave the camp without a guard escort or a policeman. It felt strange walking around without the enemy being around. I didn't find anything of note, but should mention that I came to a shop (bar) where seven out of ten men partook of whiskey and a glass of lemonade. I had much fun during my short sojourn. We also had Holtzhuizen from our tent admitted to the hospital.

Wednesday 30th April. I went out to the barracks to fetch a clothing issue. We each got 2 underpants, 1 shirt, 2 vests, 1 towel, and 2 handkerchiefs and luckily I got a pair of shoes. In the afternoon I felt very indisposed with a migraine headache

Thursday 1st May 1902. Nothing significant to report. One of the cook houses caught alight, with much damage. I set my school teaching time from 2 till 4 o'clock in the afternoons seeing the days are so hot. We are informed verbally that Peace had been concluded in South Africa. We would wait till the morning to get confirmation. We gathered from a letter from Sister Bettie to P. Meyer that our family are still okay.

Friday 2nd May. Our dear late Hettie's birthday – in the late afternoon I had another migraine, which troubled me the whole night.

Saturday 3rd May. I gratefully received the first letter from my brother Pieter who was paroled from Bhim Tal camp. I wrote a letter to Uncle A. Geldenhuys at the Bellary Camp. Peace talks are doing the rounds. J. Rabie who we nicknamed Ou Booi is pleasant and excited. My Father-in-law Abram and I bought a bottle of milk for 1 anna (1 Penny) and with some rice which we had, we made a tasty supper.

Sunday 4th May. I have just returned from the Barracks! Oh how sinful to see the Indians carry on with their work on the Sabbath. Apparently no distinction is made between a Sunday and a Monday. I wrote a second letter to brother Pieter, seeing that I was rather hard on him yesterday regarding accepting parole from the enemy. Our Indian cook prepared our meal. Father Preller held the morning service and the evening church were conducted by Captain Bosch. The reading was taken from 1 Samuel 22, with the sermon focusing on verse 16. The day was again hot and unpleasant. Another tent joined ours for home cell in our tent. I together with another from our tent excused us from the prayer meeting as one of the newcomers would make a mockery of the prayer meeting by praying occasionally non-stop for half an hour.

Ernst van Biljon, Jan Geldenhuys and Abram Preller

Monday 5th May. It is again my turn to be on duty at the tent. I made one neck-tie depicting the Free State colours, which I intend showing off when I return there. I experience severe longing for our loved ones separated by thousands of miles, but were consoled by the fact that, God willing, we would be reunited before long. I needed to get a pass to collect the portrait that was taken of us, from the photographer in town. I also went to the hospital to get treatment / medicine for a rash that I was getting on my hands. I also saw the friend from our tent who was in the hospital and was pleased to notice that he was on the mend.

Tuesday 6th May. I made application to collect the portrait in town but permission was not granted because the Camp Major was absent. This was a big disappointment, having done all the preparation and arrangements. I then wrote a letter to my sister Bettie. We then cooked a large pot of 4lb of ginger jam and then cooled and placed it on the table to thicken. The day is particularly hot, practically impossible for anyone to venture outside the tent. J. Rabie is not feeling too well as he was suffering from a sore throat. I teased him to shave off his moustache.

Wednesday 7th May. I took the whole day to make a bow tie, which attracted the attention of all the tent inmates. Apart from that, nothing else of note happened baring Rheeder who took a catnap in the afternoon. When he woke up and put on his spectacles the metal nose-bridge was just too hot from the sun that he had no option but to take his spectacles off until wearing it became more bearable. This gives the reader an idea of just how hot it can become in India. During the morning I went to the hospital to inspect for vaccination against chicken pox. I was alright but those who had not been previously treated required them to be vaccinated.

Thursday 8th May. Although the day was not as hot as yesterday, it was very windy and dusty. I made a cigar holder out of one buffalo horn which will provide future memories of our stay in India. A number of the tent inmates have been transferred to the barracks and quite a few peace-talk stories are doing the rounds - - fuelled by several persons who had received letters from South Africa. In the afternoon my father-in-law Preller, Ernst (van Biljon) and I were privileged to enjoy a decent bath. Johannes Rabie (Ou Booi) made supper for us – dumplings from corn-meal which we get from the British Government on Sundays and Thursdays, in lieu of rice, which makes an appetising change to our diet. All the old folk and young children were instructed to report to the main gate at 06h00 the next morning, for transfer to the cooler mountainous camp.

Friday 9th May. As we marched out to the Commissariat, we passed a new batch of inmates marching to Camp Umballa. The newcomers were issued with one pair of pants, a pair of navy blue shoes and a pair of slippers for night use as walking barefoot was just too unhealthy. After having left the camp, about 500 paces, we came across a large gathering of Indians carrying flags and beating drums. We are told by others that the Indians are holding some sort of religious worship to cattle, which they consider to be sacred.

It is our tent's turn to hold the evening prayer-meeting, which is conducted by father-in-law Preller – who takes his reading from Acts 1st Chapter – and asks God to show his mercies to us as well as the Indian heathen.

The Camp Major who had been away for eight days, would surely issue us a pass to fetch the portraits that we had had taken.

Saturday 10th May. We enjoy a particularly cool and pleasant day. E. van Biljon has terrible toothache. I sympathised with him seeing that I myself had a similar experience. My duty for the day is to shorten the khaki trousers that I had received yesterday. I spent the time to cut off the necessary length and then sowed the hems. I stopped teaching in view of all the children having left for the cooler mountainous camp. I need to end as the bugle has sounded lights out.

Sunday 11th May. It is my turn to stand on duty outside the tent. We had had a nice bout of rain during the night. Despite heavy thunderstorms, the air smelled very fresh and appeared very clean with good visibility all round. For breakfast I made yellow mealie meal and milk. We purchase the mielies for one paai, which is one farthing. For dinner we had mutton with potatoes, and soup made from meal, potatoes and onions. Father Preller conducted the church service, which helped to pass the time. I wrote a letter to my father. Ernst went to the doctor to extract his troublesome tooth, after five failed attempts, with Ernst being in dreadful pain. With my own experience I empathised seeing the doctor had failed to extract the tooth completely. I warmed a Dixie over the lamp and placed it on his cheek to help soothe the pain. I also smeared the gum with lamp oil and some pain-killer, which seemed to help somewhat. I decided to give the general church service a miss and rather stayed behind to console my friend.

Monday 12th May. Another very pleasant day. We appealed to our Captain to approach the Major about our ration of milk, jam and tobacco, like we used to be issued with when we first arrived at Umballa. However, once the burgers refused to take advantage of the parole offered, the ration was stopped. We are advised that parole can still be taken and that the ration of milk, jam and tobacco would be issued. We declined, preferring to suffer the heat and hunger than to make concessions. I busied myself with making neck ties all day. Captain Eberson conducted the general church service, preaching from Mark 13 (freedom being imminent). I decided to wait till the morning to apply for permission to fetch our portrait.

Tuesday 13th May. I obtained a Pass from the Major to go into the Umballa Township, from 9 o'clock p.m. till 7 am. Those granted permission were A. Preller, F. Brewis, M. van Biljon, Gert van der Merwe, N. Schalkwyk and I. En route we came across four elephants, driven by Indians. It cost us one Anna (one penny) for the ride. The others were rather sceptical, but I found the experience out of this world and was sorry that the others were just too afraid to do the elephant ride. We got our portraits from the photographer and then continued on to the bazaar. The Bazaar was quite fascinating, consisting mainly of many small stalls selling all sorts of goods and services. I purchased one span speck for 3 (rupees?), about 3 farthings – identical to the delicious taste as in South Africa. At Eramju's shop we bought our dinner of salmon and biscuits. We then proceeded to Saint Paul's church and upon entering we noticed crosses and candelabra similar to ours. We climbed the church tower which rose to about 100 feet high, which gave good views of the whole of Umballa. When we got down we decided to return to the camp. Natan and I found a buggy and paid 12 Annas or one shilling to travel around for one hour. We visited the race course and the railway station before returning to the camp, where had managed to smuggle in an half-jack of whiskey for my sick friend E. van Biljon, whose toothache prevented him from accompanying us earlier. It had been a long day, and I was quite tired.

Wednesday 14th May. During last night we had a rather rare event. A jackal came into our tent at about 11 o'clock, jumped onto the table and walked around where seven persons are sleeping. My father frightened him off. I got a letter from P. Colin Meyer who wrote that he had received word from Sister Bettie in which all was well at home, including good news from my beloved wife. The glad tidings also brought on longing for family that were separated from one another. God willing, I look forward to reading his letter myself. He told me that he had received a letter from my brother Pieter as well, of the 4th inst. and that it is still well with him and my father. Old Jacobus van den Berg, who had been admitted to hospital a month ago with measles, was discharged. He said that a troop had told him that we were to leave the camp on the 15th because 50 000 troops were arriving from South Africa. He also said that we had lost our independence. The closer we got to the 15th, the more the peace terms circulated. I made labels for us, to attach to our bundles of belongings, in anticipation of us leaving the camp. Father Preller is not feeling too well and Roll Call is postponed till half-past nine, the reason being that the church duties needed to be stored. Old Natan received a letter from his brother and tried to persuade him to consider taking the parole. He his highly distraught seeing this is the second time that he maintained taking parole was out of the question.

Thursday 15th May. I went to the Major to get a Pass to see Piet Meyer so that I could get hold of the letter that my sister Bettie had written him. To my consternation I found the Major so drunk that he could hardly stand on his feet, and not knowing his left from his right. It is disgusting for an Afrikaner to behave in such a state in a foreign country. Jan Venter was with me when we went passed the Indian Government offices. We saw a beautiful pair of horses, imported from Australia. We also witnessed another shameful event when our neighbouring tent who had been given a pass into Umballa and returned in a very inebriated state. Father Preller is quite sickly. I prepared a concoction of warm ginger with a dram of whisky. The day is pleasantly overcast with the likelihood of rain in the offing. I wrote a letter to Uncle Hennie Schikkerling hoping that he would receive it speedily.

Friday 16th May. During the morning I went to the hospital to get ointment for a burn that I got from the lamp glass. I met up with our friend Holtzhuizen who is in hospital and hopeful of a speedy recovery. He summarised the news circulating in the camp and from letters got from South Africa. It is apparent that:-

1. Yesterday about 200 Boers passed the camp and dropped off a parcel for one of the camp inmates.
2. The Major had said that we were not to be surprised if suddenly instructed to leave for another camp.
3. Meyer had told me that an Englishman had said that Peace Talks had been concluded in South Africa.
4. One letter from Africa to say that the yellow checked dog had had puppies but did not survive giving birth to all the very scrawny offspring – but that the black dog was very fat and aggressive, wanting to bite everything in sight.
5. Grandpa and Grandma got married and were waiting for the children to wish them well - - and that Grandpa's

children will inherit everything, but not Grandma's children.

Lizzie Geldenhuys

3-months old Hettie died in the Kroonstad Concentration camp

Paardeberg monument – forms a cross when viewed from the air

Boer memorial – Bloemfontein Vroue Museum

The author with his wife Rina Geldenhuys in front of the Afskeid monument

Delene McColl (nee Geldenhuys) – Kroonstad museum

Kroonstad church and Boer War monument

Magersfontein summit

DIT NATIONAAL MONUMENT
IS OPGERICHT
TER NAGEDACHTENIS AAN DE
26370 VROUWEN EN KINDEREN
DIE IN DE CONCENTRATIEKAMPEN
ZYN OMGEKOMEN
EN AAN DE ANDERE
VROUWEN EN KINDEREN
DIE ELDERS TENGEVOLGE
VAN DEN OORLOG 1899-1902
ZYN BEZWEKEN

Powerful inscription at the Vroue Monument - Bloemfontein: 26 370 women and children die in the Concentration Camps during the 1899 - 1902 war

Durban City Hall

Kimberley Long Cecil named after Cecil John Rhodes, the founder of Rhodesia

Die Bittereinde - The Bitter End

Typical laager – perfected at Blood River

Bloemfontein and Paardeberg monuments

Voortrekker Museum, Winburg – now hijacked by Winnie Mandela

MAGERSFONTEIN BURGHER MONUMENT

Burials at this monument have taken place on three different occasions. Those who died of wounds at the Boer casualty station (then Bissett's farm) across the road; those re-interred during the late 1920's and commemorated on the memorial standing under the apex of the monument; and those re-interred during the 1960's from areas within a radius of about 100 km thereof.

The monument was designed by Bosman and Smal Architects and unveiled in 1969. The four sides of the pyramid represent the union of the four provinces, while the three spaces between the eastern columns symbolise the three years of the war. From above the memorial appears as a perfect cross.

Amongst the casualties buried here are Adriaan de la Rey, eldest son of Gen J.H. de la Rey; the French Colonel, the Comte de Villebois-Mareuil; Scandinavian volunteers; a lone British soldier and a woman, Nurse Combrinck.

Magersfontein Burger Monument inscription

Rustpan – in 1968 and 2008

To whom it may Concern

We, the undersigned, hereby leave a few statements to those surviving ourselves and who may in coming generations recover this paper.
This document was [illegible] on its [illegible] the house of Jan A. Geldenhuys on his farm Rustpan on the 8th of April, 1920 ad.
The weather is very promising; in the West a heavy thunderstorm is brewing. The mealies are growing beautifully. The sheep have started lambing.
~~There is a school on the farm~~
With kindest wishes to the world at large, we remain
your ancestors:-

J. J. A. Geldenhuys
(wife) Lissie Prellar.
Family:- Henry Geldenhuys
Bessie Geldenhuys
Lettie Geldenhuys
[illegible]
Klembaas Prellar.
H Douwes (Teacher.)

Rustpan,
Dist. [illegible]
8th April, 1920.

The letter, now nearly 90 years-old, recovered from a sealed bottle buried in the walls of Rustpan's homestead built by Jan Geldenhuys

Johannes Albertus Geldenhuys – Rustpan, Bothaville
Born 8 July 1877 – Died 28 May 1944

The authors grandparents' graves on Rustpan Farm, Bothaville

6. The red grasshoppers are plentiful, and also ticks.
7. Grasshoppers are diminishing while chameleons are increasing.
8. News reports are that farmers are fleeing to Madagascar and Rhodesia.
9. A letter of a women to her brother pleading that he remain loyal to Uncle Paul (President Kruger) and that he should not allow him to be mislead.

To my dismay I need mention a certain person in our tent that speaks ill of all our women and female children and is surprised that he managed to smuggle something so war sensitive into the camp.

This morning all the old folk and children received a bag and string, with ticket attached, to relocate to the mountainous camp in eight days time. We also received gift parcels from Holland consisting of half-a-pound tobacco, a box of matches, five cigarettes and one and a half ounces cheese. The tobacco, which is in short supply in the camp, was well received, especially for those without financial means to support their habits. Our names were called for the periodic bath, which we thoroughly enjoyed in the afternoon. Peace talks are plentiful. I hired Rheeler, at the cost of five cigarettes, to do my tent duty the next day.

Saturday 17th May. I received two letters from South Africa – one from my mother and the second from my sister Bettie. My spirit was raised and I am truly grateful to our heavenly Father who cares for their welfare. O, what joy to get news from my beloved wife Meidje. Bettie says that it is still well with her. I answered both letters immediately. Last night 770 soldiers arrived from South Africa, amongst which were several Afrikaners. Old people are instructed to depart the next day. I read a letter which a sister had written to her brother to read Psalm 126 with Ezegh 36, below which she mentioned that, Grandpa and Grandma has an argument. Ouma wanted to wear the trousers so Oupa gave her a hiding and now he is ‘king of his castle”! Ouma is depicted as the British, and Oupa the Boer!

Sunday 18th May. Roll call is done on old people's baggage, which is loaded and carted my mules to the railway station. Some of the old men refused to relocate to the cooler mountainous areas and are placed in jail like old Z. Prinsloo and M. Rautenbach. We found lamb but the meat was unfit for human consumption. We would find out later what happened to it. About 6 o'clock the old men and children were taken to Salon and it was sad to see them bid farewell to their family and friends, many of whom came with us from South Africa. In the evening a prayer meeting was held in our tent, conducted by Pa Preller. The subject was to pray for the speedy recovery of our hospitalised brethren, here as well as in Africa. John, Chapter 11 was read. Corporals were ordered to empty the tents as new inmates were due to be accommodated.

Monday 19th May. I received on letter from my father (H. Geldenhuys) and was pleased to learn that it was still well with him. We were moved to another tent.

Tuesday 20th May. We pitched our tent before the arrival of the new burgers. The day is again hot and sticky. I bought a piece of canvas for six Annas, planning to use it for the journey to South Africa. I patched and darned one pair of socks for my Father-in-law Abram, ensuring that a good and proper job was made.

Wednesday 21st May. Early morning the bugle was sounded before the normal Roll-call. When we fell in the Sergeant came and marched us to the gate and herded us into a small enclosure. The police lieutenant then went into our camp to search through our belongings. It was dreadful to see how our goods were strewn all over the place – with the police confiscating what little money and cigarettes they could find. They discovered one solitary ammunition round. While we were rounded up and detained in the small enclosure, the new prisoners of war arrived from the station. We soon met up with many of our friends like N. Meyer, C. Smit, N. Boshof, and butcher P. Marais from Klerksdorp. C. Smit informed me that 15 days after I was captured, he had seen my dear wife and said it was still well with her. Oh, what glad tidings it was to learn of our beloved back home. We also met up with Uncle Bennie van Biljon who told us much about S.A. One of the new arrivals died of sun-stroke. The day is extremely hot. After the bugle was blown for Roll-call, the Sergeant said that anyone who wished to attend the funeral should assemble the next morning at a ¼ to 6 at the gate. I wished to attend, God willing.

Thursday 22nd May. Father Preller, E van Biljon and I, from our tent went to the funeral. We were escorted by an armed guard to the hospital mortuary where pall-bearers were called for. Ernst and I volunteered and placed the corpse on the gun carriage. The immediate family of the deceased were also carted on the canon, drawn by six beautiful horses, to the cemetery. The Sergeant instructed the bearers to position either side of the gun-carriage, up to the grave side. The burial was conducted by the English padre. After the body was lowered into the grave, a firing squad fired off three-gun salutes, during which the death-march was played. After the burial, we returned to the camp. During the afternoon, father Preller received word from the hospital that another burger that had just arrived had died, and would be buried in the morrow.

Friday 26th May. Sections I to 4 moved into the barracks. It was an unpleasant day with much wind and dust flying around. It was feared that the house would cave in. It was my turn to stand in front of our tent. I got a poem which was very apt and wrote it down as follows:

The Poem

(The poem – translated)

In cities and towns and everywhere
Sorrow replaces joy
The weeping mother and screaming child
To father
Quivering grey-head
Brings tragic news; the telegram reads
Died for Freedom and Righteousness
He hoists the banners
To our living heroes fighting the battles
Stricken and shedding blood

Storms the enemy strongholds with fervour
The battle outcome is in the Lords hands
Drying tears after each encounter
For Freedom and Righteousness
Striking mothers cease weeping
And wipe your tears

The dying heroes
We lay down our lives for the Lord
We lay down our lives for the Lord
Expecting our support and seeking honour
And graves proclaim
Our motto remains for Freedom and Righteousness

Also appropriate was the scripture from Psalm 146 versus 3-7

We received news from a telegram saying that six of our officers from the Vereeniging Conference were dispatched to Pretoria amongst which were generals de Wet and de le Rey.

Saturday 24th May. During the morning the lieutenants are told that Peace had been concluded. The message is later conveyed to the Major and Adjutant. May the good Lord uphold truthfulness.

Sunday 25th May. I received a portrait in which my father, my brother Pieter, Uncle Hennie Schikkerling, Uncle Jan Steyn and with six other persons. It was a relief to see their faces but it grieved me to see that Khaki was photographed right in the middle of the group. I wrote a letter to my father thanking him for the portrait. Peace rumours are becoming more heated.

Monday 26th May. We went out on a route march during the morning, but on returning the weather turned and a terrific wind came up, followed by a welcome rain shower. However, one barrack was blown down. However, after the thunderstorm the day cooled down quite a lot and in fact turned out as one of our most pleasant day's to-date at Umballa.

Tuesday 27th May. A 9-inch square Freedom flag was circulated in the camp. Captain Boshof took ill and was admitted to hospital – with Corporal Heckrood appointed in his stead.

Wednesday 28th May. I went to the hospital to collect Capt Boshof's clothes. En route, a policeman told me that we will be returned speedily to Africa and that one of these days canon fire will sound a salute to peace.

Thursday 29th May. I received a newspaper in which it said that tomorrow was King Edward's birthday, which will be widely celebrated in India. However, to my knowledge his birthday is in October!

Friday 30th May. The English held a marching parade and general salute with canons to commemorate the kings birthday. One of the British soldiers committed suicide by shooting himself with a rifle.

Saturday 31st May. A tobacco issue was handed out. I got about half-a-pound. The Major informed us that we were now permitted to write letters here in India and to South Africa without needing stamps to do so. We are also notified to expect another shipment of 160 Boer prisoners from South Africa, due to arrive tomorrow.

Peace Declaration

Monday 2nd June 1902. The Boer prisoners from Africa arrived at 08h00. I did not recognise any acquaintances, except for old Uncle Kootje Jordaan who told me that my dear Meidje had been removed from Klerksdorp by the enemy but that a M. Rademeyer had received a letter from his family saying that she had applied to the authorities to go to Kroonstad. I wrote to letters, one addressed to Klerksdorp and the other to Kroonstad. There is much excitement amongst the inmates. Some of the English officers told us that Peace had been concluded and that we could expect to return to S.A. within a month. One of the telegrams said that the British have allowed the Boers to keep their weapons as protection from marauding Blacks and wild animals, like the long-haired jackal. In the late afternoon one of our tent mates Holtzhuizen was discharged from hospital, having fully recovered.

Tuesday 3rd June. It was again my turn to serve in front of the tent. For dinner I made dumplings which turned out very tasty. Talks doing the rounds are how soon we would return to our Fatherland.

Wednesday 4th June. The Peace Conditions were telegrammed to the camp. The Boers are required to lay down their arms, surrender all their ammunition and guns and that Colonial Burgers would be banned for life and Colonial Officers would be hanged. The stories are rejected out of hand. We packed our meagre belongings so that we would be ready to leave at a moment's notice. The weather took a turn for the worse in the late afternoon.

Thursday 5th June. Rheeler was discharged from the hospital and visited us briefly, saying that he would return in order to care for the sickly. I received a letter from Sarah Geldenhuys, which she had written on the 5th April. Ernst got a letter informing him that his wife and two youngest children had died. He was devastated trying to read the tragic news. The day is otherwise quite cool and pleasant. A meeting had been held last night, at which it was decided to hold a thanksgiving and thank God for peace and deliverance. I repaired the floor to our house to make it more habitable.

Ernst van Biljon. His wife Kitty died while interned in the Klerksdorp Concentration Camp

Ernst wife Kitty had four children – who were with Oumam Lizzie in the Klerksdorp concentration camp at that time. She caught a dreadful cold and died four days after being admitted to the hospital. The surviving children were collected by Chris van Biljon and taken by train to the Prinsloo family living in

Pretoria. This picture of Ernst was taken just before he received the news of the death of his wife and children].

Saturday 6th June. After Roll-call, we moved into our house, having arrived at this camp two months ago, and having to endure the hot sun, wind and dust. I received four letters, two from my father, one from Pieter and one from Uncle Hennie – and another from sister Schikkerling. I answered all the letters. An auction was held in the camp. Dawie de Wet sold all his shop stock. Ii met the Major in the evening. He jokingly said that within a few days he would send us to the cooler mountainous camp, I replied that I would rather return to Africa. He said that he was currently busy with making arrangements and awaiting orders for our return, but was weary that we would take up arms again as soon as we got back to S.A. I asked him whether we would have to fight with sticks but he replied that the Boers would re-arm themselves. I told him we needed to shoot wild buck, not of the Khaki buck kind!

Monday 9th June. Within half an hour the weather worsened, and rain came down in buckets, pouring down on both sides. I got a letter from my father which I replied to. I also wrote to Sister Bettie. Uncle Hans de Klerk received a letter from his wife who said the family was still well. Also tidings that widow C. Engelbreg had died.

Friday 13th June. I got a letter from my father saying that he had received a telegram about the Peace, and that ships were being prepared to take us back.

Saturday 14th June. Ernst van Biljon went to the hospital to attend to an abscess in his ear. Gert and van Schalkwyk are also sickly and I gave them a tonic for their fever, trusting that they would be better by the next day. We are told that the three last people would arrive and that we were to report to the office at 6 o'clock.

Sunday 15th June. Gert van der Merwe went to the hospital. We are summoned to the office and interviewed one at a time. We were questioned to give up, whether married or not, where ones wife was, how many children and where born, how many livestock and fixed property. Fourteen of us refused to offer up anything. I reported that I could not answer except that I had a lot of livestock but could not give an accurate figure. I wrote a letter to Bettie and another to my father.

Monday 16th June. We are told that the Peace conditions would arrive in the camp tomorrow. The day is unpleasant with the wind blowing for the past three days. Some days it is so bad that one could not distinguish the sun from the moon. Hendrik van der Merwe died in the morning and was buried in the afternoon.

Tuesday 17th June. Another Boer prisoner died – H. van Aswegen.

Wednesday 18th June. Newspaper reports state that parole people take note to return to their previous camps, and those prisoners of war would be required to take the Oath of Allegiance while still in India. Bearing that in mind I wrote to my father to apply to return to Umballa. We received news that 1000 women from the Kroonstad camp would be required to go to East London. The day is unpleasant with much dust. I got my four pound tobacco and cut it up for my journey to Africa. We are all longing for the moment to be told that we are leaving this place. May the dawn arrive for me and my co-prisoners of war to be re-united with our loved ones that have been separated by thousands of miles. May God our Father grant us the strength and patience to wait the moment of the appointed time.

Thursday 19th June. We are visited by eight Indian Officers, lead by one white officer, who asked me to accompany them around the camp. One Hollander came into the camp to convey the good news which was spread at the evening prayer meeting chaired by my Father-in-law Abram. The subject of his talk was to be grateful for the Peace declaration and pray for a speedy return to our beloved fatherland.

Friday 20th June. We had lovely rains during the night, despite some of the mud constructed buildings crumbling as a result of the soaking rain. The inhabitants were forced to flee to the thatched huts. It was our turn to carry out a route march which was most welcome despite the wet conditions which did not bother us. I made a ring from tiger bone, with O.V.S. (Orange Free State) engraved on it. It came out well. I also used a marrow-bone which I personally had eaten the meat off it. We also received the formal Peace Conditions thus;

No 26728

Office of Quarter Master General in India

Army Headquarters.

Simla 13th June 1902

Miscellaneous – B

To – The Lieutenant General Commanding the Forces

Bengal, Madras P. Bombay.

Memorandum, The following telegram, dated London 9th June 1902. Summarising the terms of surrender of the Boers contained in a document signed 31st May 1902 has been received by his Excellency Viceroy the Right Honourable Secretary of State for India.

Lord Kitchener & Lord Milner on behalf of the British Govt & General C.R. de Wet, Judge J.B. Hertzog, I. Brebner & General C. Olivier, acting as Govt of the Orange Free State & S.W. Burger, M.W. Reitz, General Louis Botha, J.S. de Le Rey, Lucas Meyer, Krogh, acting as Govt of the South African republic on behalf of their respective burghers.

To terminate the present hostilities, agree on the following articles:

(1) Burgher forces will lay down arms, give up all munitions of war & desist from further resistance to the authority of his Majesty King Edward whom they recognise as their Lawful Sovereign.

(2) All burghers in and beyond the Units of the Transvaal or Orange River Colony & all Prisoners of war at present outside South Africa, who are burghers will on duly declaring their acceptance of the position of subjects, of His Majesty King Edward V11 be gradually brought back to their homes as soon as transport can be provided & their means of subsistence ensured.

(3) Burghers surrendering will not be deprived of personal liberty or property.

(4) No proceedings to be taken against burghers surrendering for bona fide acts of war except in the case of certain acts notified to Boer Generals by Commander in Chief.

(5) Dutch Language to be taught in schools when parents desire it & to be used in Law Courts where necessary.

(6) Possession of rifles for their protection to be allowed to persons taking out licence.

(7) Civil Govt. to be introduced as soon as possible followed by representative institutions leading to self Govt.

(8) No special land tax in the Transvaal or Orange River Colony to pay for war.

(9) His Majesty Govt. will set aside 3-million sterling for restoration of population to their homes & making good war losses bona fide. Possession of commandeering receipts of S.A.R.C. notes will be taken as evidence of war, loses, In addition H.M. Govt. will make advances on loan to burghers for same purposes Ends, 2 His Excellency the Commander in Chief that the substance of the fair going terms of surrender, be carefully & clearly explained to all those Prisoners of War now in India thereby affected & at the same time they be informed that owing to the denuded state of the country, some time must elapse before all of them, who fulfil the conditions therein in Posed can be sent back, but that arrangements for their gradual return will be commenced as early as possible.

By Order

Gen Henry Major General

Quarter Master General in India.

Saturday 21st June. There was much discussion during the night and in the morning. Roll-Call was held in the houses and it was my turn to do house duty. It was a pleasant, cool day. Section 1 went out for their clothing issue and instructed that it was on hold till further notice. I washed my own clothes fearing that should I give it to the Indians to do it may well remain behind since departures from here are expected from Monday onwards. Now-a-days longing for our fatherland intensifies. We experience a lovely thunderstorm during the night.

Sunday 22nd June. Our Section Capt Boshof summoned us to attend the service conducted by Viljoen. I received a letter from Uncle A. Geldenhuys which I answered immediately. Rabie went to the hospital and reported that Gert van der Merwe was very sick but that Ernst van Biljon would more than likely be discharged tomorrow. He also mentioned that the doctor had told Rheeler that the camp restrictions would be lifted by the Major in accordance with a telegram he had received.

Monday 23rd June. A swarm of bees was in the camp and stung quite a few people – many walking around with swollen eyes, cheeks and lips. I took Ernst his clothes for his discharge from the hospital. The rest of the day was taken up reading a story book. I also extracted a front tooth for my Father-in-law Abram.

Tuesday 24th June. Our Rose celebrates her birthday today. My Father-in-law Abram made us pancakes for supper. We were instructed to report to the gate at half-past six in the morning.

Wednesday 25th June. The Commissioner issued each of us with trousers and a jacket, which fell on me to do all the necessary sowing adjustments - - widening the trousers and cutting the legs shorter, doing the hems and sowing on extra pockets in the jackets since they only have one pocket. Tobacco was also issued, everyone getting one pound. Tomorrow is the Kings crowning – but rumours suggest that it may be postponed. I received a letter from my father, saying all is well. We got further news that Gert van der Merwe is very sick in hospital.

Friday 26th June. I received two letters from sisters Bettie and Maria that my father had forwarded from Bhim Tal. The letters were dated 6th May 1902. Unfortunately, I lost my July diary but I did apply on 3rd July to visit my father at Bhim Tal to celebrate our birthdays. 18 days passed to get an answer, permission granted. But I had to take parole beforehand. On 22nd July at 7 o'clock I left Umballa for Bhim Tal. The following day at 12 o'clock I arrived at Kathkodam (Kathgotlam?) station where I had to hire a horse for 2 ?, for the 8 mile journey to the camp. I was most surprised climbing the frightening mountain passes so narrow as to allow only a horse rider and a footpath that took two hours to negotiate. About half an hour before my arrival, I asked the Sergeant to send early warning to my father. About half a mile from the camp I had one unbelievable reunion with my father, brother Pieter and Uncle Hennie who I had not seen for two years. We embraced each other can for at least a quarter of an hour could not utter one word! We continued on to the camp where I met many friends who surrounded me and anxiously enquired about their family and friends. Fathers, brothers, friends and family/ all eager for news. Very topical was expected returns to S. Africa, and who had signed the Declaration. Debates raged all day long, from morning till night.

Oudad Jan's brother Pieter, who was a POW in the Trichenopoly and Bhim Tal Camps. The brothers had not seen one another for two years

The break of nearly a month, from 26 June to 23 July 1902 remains unexplained.

Whilst at Bhim Tal all the inmates were required to sign the Declaration on **24th July 1902**. On that date Pieter and I rode horseback 10 miles from Bhim Tal and noticed some of the best and clean farms in the country. The nearest town has a fair amount of white inhabitants, beautiful shops and buildings and a lovely lake to the west with boats and canoes. We lingered till about 4 o'clock before returning to Bhim Tal.

Sunday 27th July. I attended the church service which was conducted by a Dominee. It was a pleasant change to be administered to by a different Reverend, with the closing hymn taken from Gesang 78, verses 10-11 and 12 – very appropriate to our circumstance. Pieter and I then went and climbed in the mountains. We were caught in a rainstorm and arrived back at the camp drenched from head to toe. The first couple of nights that I was with my father and Pieter, we had hardly any sleep.

With about 200 other bodies we spoke of our experiences since last we had laid eyes on one another.

Tuesday 5th August 2002. Several Boers left for South Africa, at their own cost. They had obtained written permission from Sencor.

Wednesday 6th August. At 12 o'clock I left Bhim Tal, arriving back at Umballa at 4 o'clock the next morning. I caught a cab from the station and arrived at the camp while it was still dark. As I got to the main gate a security guard called out aloud: "Halt! Who is there?" For a moment I could not answer but muttered "Friend". He replied: "Pass friend - - All is Well!" After allowed in I proceeded to our bungalow and found all my old friends absent, except for my old friend Ernst van Biljon. He said that Rabie, Rheeler, van Schalkwyk and Holtzhuizen had signed the Declaration and had been transferred to the Parole Camp. We had much news to share having been separated for 15 days. I was most surprised to be told that the Burghers had come to the conclusion that it was better to sign the Declaration despite their earlier belief not to do so. It seemed that the dog that barks the loudest has a feeble bite. I then went to the hospital to see my Father-in-law Abram, who was still in the same condition than when I had left – with water still on the knee.

Friday 8th August. I went to the office and got a permanent pass to permit me to leave the camp every day. I also got a pass to allow the photographer in the camp to take a picture of our bungalow. I then told my Father-in-law Abram who said that he would be present tomorrow, and asked him what sort of flowers I should get to place on the table. Several of our friends left for South Africa in the evening – at their own cost – amongst who was Post, B. Tromp, Uncle Hansie Moolman, Danie de Wet (who has sold out his shop), and another six. The officers of the camp are in high spirits and issued us with a case with milk, meal, potatoes and promised to get us jam, which we had not had before now. I received a postcard from my sister Bettie, dated 18th June 2002.

Saturday 9th August. The photographer arrived, as did my Father-in-law Abram, from the hospital. Ernst and I had tidied up the room and decorated the mantelpiece with a photo of my father with Pieter, another of my mother with child and my dear Meidje at her side. Father had brought flowers from the hospital and these were put on the mantel piece. I spent the afternoon doing business with the photographer, promising him to obtain a pass for him to enter the Camp and to take photographs. The day is also marks the Coronation of King Edward [spelt Eduard], with the 'Reds' firing canon shot after canon salute. The Indians held a fireworks display in the evening. I wrote a letter to my brother Pieter, recommending that he apply to visit us on **Sunday, 10 August**.

In the morning Ernst and I went to see the photographer to enquire how the portrait turned out and were informed that all was well. On our return we visited my father-in-law in the hospital and then later attended the church service held by Mr du Toit of Bloemfontein. Section 1 went out to swear the oath of allegiance. We were enticed with jam to sign the declaration, but two men refused to sign – they were sent to prison for 14 days, of which seven days were rationed with rice-water.

Monday 11th August. Father was discharged from the hospital, feeling much better. The photographer arrived to take another picture. We hired Indians to cook for us, for One Rupee per quarter-day for 20 days.

Wednesday 13th August. I received a letter from my sister Bettie – dated 8 July, in which she wrote that my dearest had arrived in Kroonstad and was still in good health. I was relieved that she was amongst family who would care for one another in the event of troublesome times. I went out to the drift and met an old acquaintance Mrs Cross who always received us hospitably. She gave me seven duck eggs which I used for breakfast in the morning. I arranged to have a broach made of stone, with my beloved's name inscribed. This would serve as a reminder of the love we have for one another and enduring the hardships of our circumstance, God willing. Thy will be done. I wrote to my beloved in the belief that the letter will find her in good spirits.

Meeting Mrs Cross

Thursday 14th August. I went out to check on our photographs, and met Mrs Cross who had given me the eggs. She invited me to dinner the next day. I thanked her and said that I would be honoured.

Friday 15th August. Ernst and I went out to visit Mrs Cross. She had prepared seven different foodstuffs which we prisoners of war were totally unaccustomed to. Not only was the meal very tasty, but quite spicy and hot on the palette. Our wish was for the good Lord to bless others less fortunate than us – those still subject to hunger.

Saturday 16th August. Stock taking was held for most of the day – we were required to display tables, trunks, benches, lamps, kettles, buckets, pots and all our worldly goods in front of the tent door, in order for the quarter-master sergeant to record everything in a book. Father took note that it was thirty-nine days that he suffered pain in his legs at the hospital. Other than that the day passed peacefully.

Sunday 17th August. The church service was conducted by the Reverend Viljoen. The Christians revered the Sabbath day – not so the others who's Government treats it as just another day. The main-street in the Camp is of 'gravel' and a large iron roller is used, pulled by two very scrawny animals. Their sinews are evident of the strain taken, which is more suited to at least four oxen. Father, Ernst and I debated the circumstance, and noted that no horse, goat or sheep sounds could be heard on the Sabbath. Even the buffalo are silent. However, early morning we do hear the crowing of one chicken, and occasionally the screech of a donkey. We enjoyed a good dinner – the cook made meatballs with baked meat, potatoes, cucumber salad and the Indian even prepared a tart with a tasty filling.

Monday 18th August. I went to the Sudden Bazaar. The place was under quarantine when we first arrived, being the business hub. There were literally thousands of Indians plying their wares – resembling one very large factory. I purchased three vests for 3 Annas each. Everyone in the Camp was surprised that one could buy a vest for only 3 Annas. 14 of our Burghers left the Camp at own expense to return to South Africa.. The Camp Commandant Major notified us that we could expect repatriation to South Africa only in October – at government expense. The burgers and the Camp Police held a cricket match. The Khakis' batted first and put on a good score. Bravo to the Boere who scored better, despite a sweltering afternoon with hardly any wind around.

Tuesday 19th August. Father went with the Captains to the office to enquire as to when we could expect to return to South Africa. He could not get a straight answer, despite indications that we would be amongst the first to depart.

Wednesday 20th August. I secretly made two applications, to Breives and Corporal Möller to be sent at the earliest opportunity. This approach is kept confidential amongst a few of our friends for fear that should be become public knowledge then it would well be to our disadvantage. The Officers gave us their word that we would receive favourable consideration. This is then kept amongst ourselves so as not to cause dissatisfaction with the other Boere.

Friday 22nd August. I received two letters dated 16th August, from my father and Uncle Hennie. I went to the photographer and was disappointed that the portraits had not come out as well as expected. I wrote Pieter a letter which I posted in the evening.

Saturday 23rd August. Father, Ernst and I hired a Tom Tom – or 'Cab-Car' - for 4 Annas each for a three-hour ride. We journeyed to the Sudden Bazaar and at half-past eight we came across "Sports Games" which I estimated at between 15 and 20,000 Indians, with as many live animals the like of which I had not witnessed before in my whole life. We proceeded on to the Bazaar, and saw just as many Indians there as at the sports field.

Sunday 24th August. I woke at four in the morning. While dozing off for another quarter hour I heard a call: "Jan!" I recognised the voice but for the life of me I could not fathom why or how it would be so. Then the call came again "Jan". To my utter amazement, it was my own father standing in the doorway. Oh what joy as I called to my Father-in-law Abram and said here is my Dad – Pa [Hendrik J Geldenhuys]. We sprang out of bed and could not stop talking. On that morning of the Sabbath we were called in to the office to sign the Declaration of Allegiance. Oh what a predicament to lay on ones heart ones country and people, to abandon them.

Monday 25th August. Early morning roll-call of our names. Father, Pa and I went to the hospital, showing Pa how comfortable our facilities were compared to Bhim Tal. Pa said that in the event of him becoming sick he would apply to come to Umballa for treatment.

Tuesday 26th August. Pa, Ernst and I went out in the afternoon to look at some of the more well-to-do outlying farms, with us ending up at the Sudden Bazaar again. There we witnessed a funeral procession of one bearded 80-year old Indian. En-route to the cemetery (cremation site) the procession is led by rowdy brass band blowing bugles.

The next-of-kin are dressed in white robes and onlookers throw coins and grass on the lifeless deceased. The funeral is apparently a Hindu custom, where the relatives gather the money as the procession advances to the cremation site. The deceased is placed in a cleared circular area of about 25 yards where a large pile of logs had been collected. These logs are stacked in a heap with the body placed on top of the pile. While gun powder and grass balls are inserted everywhere, one Indian then shaves the deceased, cutting off his beard and all his hair. The body is then stripped of clothing and thoroughly washed so as to be clean for his journey to the here-after. That having been done, the body is again covered with logs and the grass set alight – to start the cremation. The fiery furnace incinerates the body until only ash remains - - that is how the Hindu handles their funerals. The funeral ritual takes about three days which is then followed by an enormous feast for the surviving relatives. This Hindu tradition made a deep impression on me which I will not forget. Even my father and Ernst were astonished.

DECLARATION OF ALLEGIANCE.

No. 30680

Ik Johannes Albertus Gelderblom | Johannes Albertus Gelderblom

(here give name, residence, sub-district and district)

Debank | Debank

Onderveldcornet | Onderveldcornet

Kroonstad ORC | Kroonstad ORC

adhere to the terms of the agreement signed at Pretoria on the 31st May between my late Government and the representatives of His Majesty's Government, and I acknowledge myself to be a subject of King Edward the VII; and I promise to own true allegiance to him, his heirs and successors according to law.

J. A. Gelderblom — Signature of the applicant. | J. A. Gelderblom — Signature of the applicant.

Declared before me at Umballa

this ___ day of August Nineteen hundred and two.

Colonel Commanding at Umballa

Signature of the Special Commissioner.

25 August 1902 – Declaration of Allegiance

Wednesday 27th August. Father (in-law), Pa and I went out in the afternoon, with one car, to a circus, where we experienced much pleasure to see how nimble and agile the Indians performers were. It was amazing to witness these spectacles.

Thursday 28th August. My brother Pieter arrived very unexpectedly at 3 o'clock. It was a joyful meeting since we were of the belief that he was still in the Bhim Tal hospital. We were glad to see that he was in good health, and thanked the

Lord for his kindness and blessings in this strange country. I went to the Commandant to report Pieter's arrival, and then took Pieter to meet Mrs Cross who had shown me compassion. She was pleased to meet Pieter and repeated my good fortune to have two fathers and a brother with me in India. She gave us a large spanspek (Mush-melon, cantaloupe, or sweet melon) which we took back to the camp. We had a pleasant rain shower and the weather continued to look very promising for more rain. When we returned to the camp we found much excitement about returning to Africa.

Friday 29th August. At half-past two 175 men were notified to return to Africa. My father-n-law was on the list but to my great disappointment my name was omitted. Our Corporal's name was on the list and this very kind and considerate man then offered his place on the list to me. I will never forget his kindness towards me and would accompany me to the office. At half-past three Corporal Heckrood came with me to approach the senior official at the office to volunteer to replace my name for his on the list. However, the stymie scoundrel would hear nothing of it. Despite going to great lengths our coaxing was futile. Pieter and I then decided to visit the church spire and about one hundred paces from it I was summoned by the Captain and asked whether I was aware that leaving the camp from 9 to 5 had been stopped. I replied that I had a pass to permit me an all day exit – and to my relief it saved me from the guardroom. My father, Pieter and I then returned immediately to the camp. Afterwards, my father approached the Captain to query whether there was any possibility of me accompanying him (back to Africa). The outcome was that a ruling would be given the next day. That raised our hopes that the outcome would be favourable. We busied ourselves packing up my father's belongings, with the hold camp being in rebellious commotion. There is also talk that a large number of Boers here in Umballa would also leave next Saturday.

Saturday 30th August. Nothing transpired getting my name on the list. At 9 o'clock we bid farewell to my Father-in-law Abram and the other Boers. I went back to the office but nothing came of it. In the late afternoon we had a lovely rain shower. I got a letter from my father-in-law to say that his walking stick was stolen while waiting for his luggage to be loaded at the railway station.

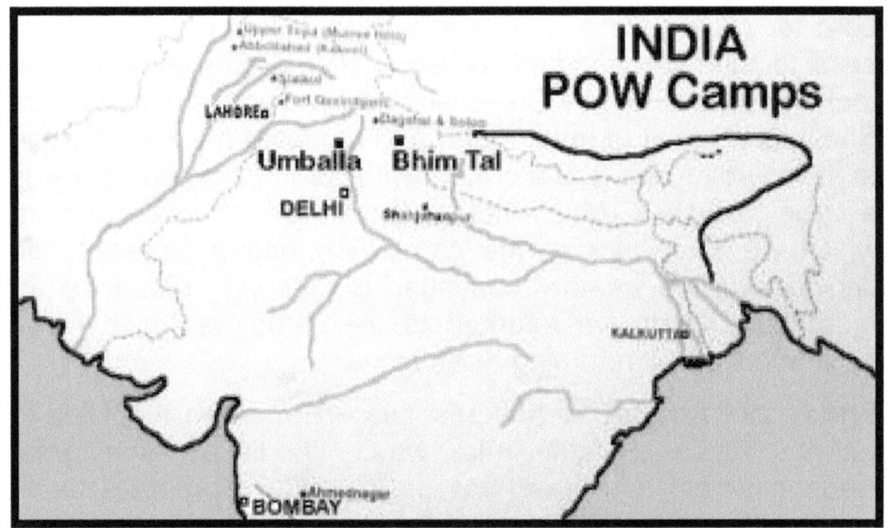

Bhim Tal and Umballa Anglo-Boer War prisoner-of-war camps, situated north and north-east of Delhi.

Sunday 31st August. After so much longing, under the circumstances, I received a letter from my Meidje dated 30th July in which she told me of the birth of our very healthy baby boy (Henry – nicknamed Oubassie), who was now one month and 18 days old. I thanked God for his everlasting kindness and blessings. Pa and Pieter on congratulated me on the birth of my son. Co-incidentally I received another letter of the same date. Pa let the church service giving thanks. That evening Pieter and I attended the Church of England service and thereafter returned to the camp.

Monday 1st September. During the morning Pieter and I were sent to collect our rations after the 'Roll Call' was held. The Captain asked me to read and call out the names. The day was extremely hot.

Tuesday 2nd September. The day was muggy and hat. In the late afternoon Pa and I went to see a show by an Indian who performed an amazing array of tricks.

Wednesday 3rd September. Pieter and I went out to try and exchange "Blue-Jacks", a sort of paper money, but were unsuccessful. Pa, Pieter, Ernst and I wanted to go for a walk in the afternoon and because of it being a very hot day we left our jackets behind. The police at the gate chased us back to fetch our jackets, which we did and so did not antagonise the guard at the gate.

Thursday 4th September. Pa and Pieter went out in the morning to request from the Commandant that they are permitted to return to Bhim Tal. I applied and was granted a pass to see them off at the railway station. We left the camp at 5 o'clock to catch the 6:30 train. We parted company with the wish to meet up again back home, God willing. At the station I met up with J van der Merwe, who was returning to Africa at his own cost. He told me there were another 34 who likewise are paying their own way and they were expected to arrive at 9 o'clock. That evening another nine Boers left the camp for Afrika, paying their own way. The day was extremely hot but with a welcome shower during the evening.

Friday 5th September. Both Ernst and I are feeling unwell. I had a bad migraine. The day was lonely because we missed the company of Pa and Pieter.

Saturday 6th September. Two Boers had a disagreement and came to blows. The result was that I scored a Bloem.

Sunday 7th September. Jan Venter arrived to request Ernst to conduct the Service, which received the sanction of the Corporal. In the evening Ernst and I paid a visit to our good friend Mrs Cross. She was very friendly and when we left she gave my eggs for breakfast and a bottle of Gooseberry jam, which I gratefully thanked her for. She said that we would have gotten more eggs but her kittens played football with them and broke a couple.

Monday 8th September. There was a thunderstorm during the night and the day was pleasant and cool. Ernst is really sick and will be admitted to the hospital tomorrow.

Tuesday 9th September. Ernst was admitted to hospital which left me without company. I spent the time going to a concert which helped to pass the time, returning to the camp at 12 o'clock.

Wednesday 10th September. I received a letter from my dear Meidje, dated 8 August, saying that she and the youngster is in good health. I also got a letter from my Father-in-law Abram to say that they had arrived at Maaras on the 4th instant. Then I also received a telegram or postal order from my father with 10 rupees which I immediately replied to thank him for the money. I then visited Ernst in the hospital and then went to the Sudden

Bazaar. On my return I got lost in Umballa and turned up at the railway station. From there I found my way back to the camp.

Thursday 11th September. I got a post card from my Father-in-law Abram boarding ship and bidding farewell to India. Then I received another blanket, over above the first Government blanket.

Friday 12th September. New orders were issued during 'Roll-Call', permitting exits from the camp by day or night, but only after the roll-call at 9 o'clock in the morning and had to be back in the camp by 9:30 in the evenings. I visited Ernst in the hospital during the afternoon, and spent the rest of the day reading – seeing there was nothing else to do but read.

Saturday 13th September. Nothing significant occurred during the day.

Sunday 14th September. I went out during the morning and had a few cups of tea with Mrs Cross and some delicious steamed pears. In the evening I visited Ernst in the hospital and also received a letter from my brother Pieter who is still well.

Monday 15th September. I spent the day alone and longing and whiled away the time reading. I included my dearest but may comment later.

Tuesday 16th September. I made up a parcel of tobacco for Pieter and went to the office for a permit to post it to Bhim Tal. The Commandant issued a pass to me and said that when I presented a postage receipt then my expenses would be reimbursed. It was dreadfully hot before midday but a thundershower in the afternoon brought much relief. I visited Ernst in hospital in the evening and found him much better.

Wednesday 17th September. I went to the office in the morning to with the postal receipt and the Commandant reimbursed my costs. Ernst was discharged from the hospital despite not fully recovered.

Friday 19th September. A lonely day was carried out – the weather was cool and pleasant.

Saturday 20th September. I got a letter from Pa and all is well with them. Four English girls and women visited the camp in the afternoon.

Sunday 21st September. Revered Mr du Toit conducted the divine worship during the morning. A few friends of mine and I went out to see the kind old lady. She prepared a nice dinner for us.

Monday 22nd September. I received two refreshing letters from my distant spouse dated 21st and 25th August.

Tuesday 23rd September. We wiled the time away making picture frames out of cigar boxes.

Wednesday 24th September. Nothing in particular took place today. Martin Rautenbach arrived.

Thursday 25th September. I did not feel too well today due to a painful headache.

Friday 26th September. We had another unpleasant day. Very windy and later quite cool. I went for a stroll in the late afternoon.

Saturday 27th September. A mournful and longing time spent. No news received from any quarter.

Sunday 28th September. Our church service is again held by Mr du Toit. In the evening I attended the Roman Catholic Church and found their customs a rarity, not having previously been to a Catholic service. I wrote a letter to my father, pleading to make provision for us to pay our own fares in order to return to Africa.

Monday 29th September. I received a letter from J van der Veen containing 10 Rupees which he would like me to buy tobacco for him. I completed his order and obtained a permit to deliver the parcel to the railway station.

Tuesday 30TH September. Ernst returned to the hospital. I took the receipt for the tobacco posting to the Commandant who duly reimbursed me for the postage. Corporal Heckrood and I went out to one of the English 'coffee shops' and were treated friendly by the 'reds' with beer etc.

Wednesday 1st October 1902. Corporal Heckrood and I were invited to a dance at the Railway Institute, for 9 O'clock. The Commandant granted us a pass-out. There were many girls, about 40 of them, who were very friendly towards us. We were permitted to mingle, eat and smoke, while Secretary Burke was present. A Mr Nathan was also present. It was a respectable

Party. The girls were tastefully dressed and mingled friendly with all the Boers. Festivities came to an end at 3 o'clock in the morning when we had to return to the camp.

Thursday 2nd October. I received a letter from my brother Pieter, in which he said all was well. I got a pass at 8 o'clock to go to the circus but en-route while passing the Northanton Coffee Shop a couple of Tommies invited us to join them. They plied us with food and drink and when well inebriated we continued to the circus, where admission was free. Seeing the elephants, tigers and apes was quite a treat. The circus was called Abell's Great Eastern Circus. When the performances ended at 12 o'clock at night the Baas Mr Abell made a speech inviting all the Boers in the camp to a special free-performance on Saturday, before returning to South Africa. All the Boers clapped their hands and made a lot of noise because of Mr Abell's sympathies for the Boer prisoners.

Friday 3rd October. I duly noted the third anniversary when the bitter conflict started that I had to bid farewell to my young bride, not knowing whether we would ever re-unite again. We thank God for his will to be done. I wrote a letter to Pieter and then visited Ernst in the hospital, finding him in good spirits.

Saturday 4th October. The circus started at 4 o'clock and was well attended by all the appreciative Boers.

Sunday 5th October. Corporal Heckrood and I went out in the morning and received the good tidings that 560 men from Umballa would depart, first 263 on the 15th October and remainder on 17th October. This brought a great upheaval in the camp, with everyone anxious to find out whether their names are on the list. Rumour has it that on Thursday people will be told who would leave on the Friday. Oh, will the day of our salvation dawn for those left behind to ever see their beloved father-land again and blessing from God to permit re-uniting with family. In the evening I visited Ernst in hospital and found him somewhat better.

Tuesday 7th October. It is now six months since my arrival in Umballa. I received a letter from my dearest Meidjie, dated 3rd September, with great relief to find out that she and our small darling are well. I then went to the office to see the head Sergeant who now knows me quite well to appeal to have my name put on the list in order to leave at the earliest opportunity.

He promised to do so. Whilst being very friendly the need for confidentiality was stressed.

Wednesday 8th October. I returned to the office to enquire whether my name was on the list but to no avail. However, by late afternoon I was told secretly by XX that my name was indeed on the list, with 30 other Kroonstaders having been omitted, but had slyly placed my name on the list. I visited Ernst in the hospital during the late afternoon and found him better than usual.

Thursday 9th October. I was alone in my thoughts expecting to be summoned but the day passed without it happening.

Friday 10th October. One great disappointment with notification my telegram that the ship that we expected has been diverted to Ceylon, with all the Boers being 'sad and heart-broken' with this turn of events. Now it is just a question of time and may that day arrive soon. The Corporal and I went to the Indian Church and found the sermon somewhat strange with the baptism of four children and one roasted sheep's head. Seems the sheep's head was accepted as a god to the Hindu's. After the religious service a feast was had by all. I wrote to Pa to inform him of my great disappointment.

Saturday 11th October. Grienes, one of the clerks in the office, who I got to know quite well, came to me in the late afternoon to tell me confidentially that he had caught sight of a telegram at midday, in which it stated that next Thursday 180 men would depart from Umballa for South Africa, and a further number on the 22nd. He promised me that he would make a plan to get my name on the list. Be it my lucky day should that happen.

Sunday 12th October. It is heart-breaking for me to think that my small son Hennie is already three months old to-day and I have not yet cast eyes on him. Our religious service is conducted by the reverend du Toit, preaching from Mark 7. In the evening I went to the Sudden bazaar where Hindus (Indians) celebrate Rammadan (Ramsimie is an idol god that they worship). Their fireworks were very impressive and Ramsimie are two large dolls made from bamboo and covered with paper, with one doll being about 20 feet tall. The festivities ended with setting the dolls alight and throwing burning embers up in the air. The newspapers carried stories of a large number of ships destined to carry the Boer prisoners back to South

Africa. The ships are named Artena, Anrenia, Mant-Rose, Loke Monitaba, all expected to dock between 22nd October till 10th December, with each ship taking on 1000 men. The first 1000 will sail on the 22nd October with the Ionian, carrying prisoners from the following camps: Kakod, Murree Hills, Dagshai, Umballa, Bhim Tal and Ahmednager.

Monday 13th October. 8 men from Dagshai arrived who will stay till the Burgers from Umballa are due to depart. I saw the Pioneer newspaper that a Mr Henry Phipps donated € 1000000 pounds for the Widows Fund in South Africa. God will bless him for his kindness towards the women and orphaned children. XX paid me a visit with the tiding that another Burgers name had been scratched out on the list and my name had been inserted.

Tuesday 14th October. I visited XX in the afternoon and gave him a pipe. He showed me a list of the Burgers who are due to leave and to my great relief my own eyes saw that my name was also on the list. I visited Ernst in the hospital and found him really weak.

Wednesday 15th October. I went to see old Mrs Cross in the evening and told her of my good fortune that God willing I will be leaving shortly. She wished me luck. She gave me a small basket as a gift for my dear spouse, and gifted me an ink pot. Both the basket and ink pot were made by Indian girls.

Thursday 16th October. I went to the artillery where 'sports' entailed high jump, pig and horse racing, etc.

Friday 17th October. I visited Ernst and found him better. In the afternoon I went to watch where the officers were playing polo. I received two letters, one from Pa and the second from Pieter, informing me of their disappointment that they were due to depart on the 15th but that the ship had been diverted to Ceylon instead.

Saturday 18th October. It is already eight months since my capture and sorrowful separation from my dearly beloved. Last night there were 40 arrivals from Kakool and 10 men from Amritsar Fort. It was a lovely cool day. I went to the hospital to visit Ernst who was only a litter better. About 9 o'clock another 85 men arrived, from Upper Topa (Murree hills).

Tuesday 21st October. There is much merriment in the camp with the anticipated arrival of the hour to leave the camp.

Wednesday 22nd October. I was instructed to report to the office at half-past six to be issued with clothing. I received one khaki jacket and a woollen sweater and told to be ready for our departure on the morrow. I went to bid Mrs Cross farewell but had to stay over for dinner. We had a nice time together and she gave me another lovely little present and wished me a speedy and safe journey. I also went to the hospital to greet my friend. 153 men arrived at 10 o'clock from Upper Topa, amongst which I re-united with several well-known persons.

Thursday 23rd October. I was told this morning to be ready at the office at 4 o'clock, with my baggage, to leave for the station. Trunks and handbags together with bedrolls are fastened together. At about 3 we went around the camp to greet our acquaintances. At 4 o'clock we assembled at the gate with our entire luggage when we got the news that our departure was being postponed to Saturday 25th. Devastated we returned again. During the day I received a letter from Pa who said that his name was not on the list. I had replied that we due to depart at 5 o'clock and I quickly went back to the postmaster to retrieve my letter.

Friday 24th October. 14 men from Umballa left at own cost for Africa. In the evening I went to Mrs Jacques who had prepared pad-kos for me the night before. She informed me of her disappointment too.

Farewell Umballa

Saturday 25th October. We were instructed at 'Roll-Call' to parade at the office at 5 o'clock with our luggage in order to march to the station. At 7 o'clock we left Umballa. Farewell Umballa!!!

Sunday 26th October. After travelling the whole night we arrived at the Rest-station. We had to wait two hours for a meal. After the food had been served, we were allocated six persons to a compartment, with handbags and trunks being sent to the hold. While boarding the train I slyly kept my trunks with me.

Monday 27th October. Last night it was up to us to settle down. There were no lights in the carriage and at 5 o'clock we arrived at Jansi where we boarded an older train – also 3rd Class but hardly cleaner than the first. Food was dished out and we were given two hours rest before departing.

Tuesday 28th October. We were transferred to another carriage, which was badly overcrowded. At 6 o'clock we arrived at Kluandwe Rest-station where half-rations were issued. We departed at 10 o'clock.

Wednesday 29th October. We arrived at Deolali rest-station at 5 o'clock, which transpired to be the best railway station that I had seen in India. Food was dished out with everyone getting half a piece ZZ. We left Deolali at 10 o'clock which gave me the opportunity to write a letter to Pa. The region is very mountainous, with us travelling trough no less than 12 tunnels over a short distance of six miles.

Thursday 30th October. We arrived in Bombay at 6 o'clock in the morning, and then boarded a tug boat to get to the ship. Hardly had we boarded ship when breakfast was served, consisting of a cup of coffee and two slices of bread. I wrote a letter to Pa to describe our travel experiences. There are 1000 men on board the ship Ionian, with an escort of 20 troops. At 2 o'clock the ship set sail from Bombay and at sunset no landfall could be seen. Everyone is excited in expectation to be re-united with our dearly beloved. We are instructed that on arrival in South Africa we would all be quarantined in a camp at Durban or Cape Town for a couple of days.

Friday 31st October. All that can be seen is the blue sea. Several passengers suffered from sea sickness, which luckily escaped me.

Saturday 1st November 1902. It is my turn to be the duty orderly at our table. The unpleasant work entailed fetching the food, washing the dishes, scrubbing the floors etc. Up to now I have been fit and strong except that I had picked up a dreadful cold.

Sunday 2nd November. A church service is held on the afterdeck of the ship. The religious sermon is conducted by a Boer from the Ahmednager camp. Before dinner I saw how the dinner was prepared. It surprised me to see how the meat was brought up, chopped into pieces and packed in filthy pans. Two bags of potatoes are cut open and dumped into a large pot – without being washed or peeled. Those eating the food have no idea how it was prepared and cooked.

Monday 3rd November. Up to now we have enjoyed calm seas.

Tuesday 4th November. I was very sick last night – body pains and feverish. I went to the doctor who gave me a good dose of medicine.

Wednesday 5th November. We traversed the equator last night at 6 o'clock in the morning. At some distance we could make out one whale who spouted a spray of water. The Captain announced that should current sailing conditions persist that we can expect to dock in Durban by Thursday night. Oh, what pleasure it would be to get back to our dear fatherland and embrace our dearly beloved waiting for our arrival.

Thursday 6th November. It is again my turn to be the orderly. I hired another man do carry out the duties in my stead.

Friday 7th November. The day reminded me of my sister Maria's birthday, without Pa. At sunset we passed the Comoro Islands and could clearly sea landfall, mountains and city lights, as we passed to the south-east.

Saturday 8th November. There is no evidence of any land seen last night. About a mile from the ship we saw another whale. Its size is likened to an ox-wagon.

Sunday 9th November. We passed another ship heading north. Another man, named Salmon Vermaak, died at 5 o'clock. His burial was held at 10 o'clock. So far we had xx deaths on board ship. The old man was 60 years old and suffered a stroke. Up until midday 12 o'clock we had sailed 3140 miles and had another 600 to go, hopefully prosperously.

Monday 10th November. At 9 o'clock a very strong wind from the south forced the sailors to lower and take down the sails. All the port-holes had to be closed because of the swells and raging waves, which in turn caused many to be sea-sick. It was dreadful to see so many men sick. By late afternoon the seas calmed somewhat and was not as bad as in the morning.

Tuesday 11th November. Although the wind had died down the sea was still very rough, making it difficult to keep ones footing while the ship rocked from side to side. It was my turn for orderly duties and I wanted to hire another person to do my work but everyone was still sea-sick. Without luck, I had to do it myself. At 10 p.m. we could make out mountains and could get a glimpse of our beloved Africa. From 10 o'clock to 9 o'clock we arrived offshore from Durban and lowered the anchor about 1½ miles out to sea.

Wednesday 12th November. We docked at 12 o'clock and had our baggage loaded onto trucks. We were treated well than when we were shipped to India. At least our 3rd Class carriages were better compared to the open coal trucks. We got to Umbilo at 3 o'clock where we given a meal. I enjoyed a splendid bath and took the opportunity to wash my dirty clothing. I dispatched a telegram to Kroonstad to advise of my arrival. I found a letter from Uncle Hennie dated 5th November in which I learnt that it was still well with my whole family. I met quite a few women from the Jacobs camp, and several men. The men are permitted to go where they wish. In our camp we were placed 8 men to a tent.

Thursday 13th November. I met A van der Linde. She came from the Merebank Women's camp to meet me. The day was extremely windy and dusty.

Friday 14th November. Early afternoon all the Transvalers were called to present their declarations. By 2 o'clock it was the turn of all the Free Staters to follow suit. The Camp Commandant issued us orders. In the afternoon I visited the Women's camp at Merebank.

There I found a sorrowful sight. Families were placed in rooms, some of the poor women had to care for others less fortunate. I spent the night with cousin A van der Linde. I was privileged to a proper bed for the first time in nine months previously to enjoy one, but to my disappointment I was attacked by so many fleas that I could not fall asleep. Never before in my life had I experienced so many fleas as at Merebank.

Saturday 15th November. I went over to see nephew Martha Bornman. She was so pleased to see me. In the afternoon I went over to the local cemetery. It was too dreadful to see how the women and children endured suffering and died for their country and people.

Sunday 16th November. I received notice that clothing was being handed out at the camp and returned immediately to our camp. Unfortunately, I arrived too late for any issues but was told that more would be handed out the next day.

Monday 17th November. It was another windy and dusty day. At 2 o'clock the names of the Transvalers were read out to return to the Transvaal, followed by the Free Staters. At 5 a.m. we left Umbilo in 3rd class carriages – with 10 men to a 'compartment'. The crowded discomfort made sleep impossible, with too much stacked on top of everything. Our luggage was carried in a separate truck and we were permitted only two Khaki blankets each. I received a letter from my dearest Meidje dated 13th November and was pleased to read that all was still well with them.

Tuesday 18th November. At 12 o'clock we passed through Pietermaritzburg and at Estcourt each man received a ration of one pound kluikers biscuits and one pound corned beef, to last 24 hours.

Wednesday 19th November. We passed the border between Natal and Transvaal. At Charleston we again received rations as per the earlier issue. Between Standerton and Heidelberg one of the carriages caught alight, causing a two-hour delay to extinguish the blasé and sort out the mess.

Thursday 20th November. At 6 p.m. we arrived in Elandsfontein, where we were transferred to open coal trucks. We left at 11 o'clock and shortly before sunset we passed over Vereeniging and at 9 p.m. in the evening we arrived at Kroonstad. I was met by my dearest wife – who was in the Kroonstad camp.

THE END

Afterword

The diary ended as abruptly as it had begun! To satisfy my curiosity, I quickly referred to my Grandmother, Oumam Lizzie's account in her Oorlogsherinneringe, War Memoirs.

Oudad Jan was so pleased to see his four-month old son Oubassie Hendrik for the first time. Oumam writes that the 8 day stay-over in Durban had dragged so slowly that she could hardly wait to see Oudad again. First priority was to christen the baby and then make application to the new government for repatriation assistance.

Oudad Jan, Oupa Abram Preller and the other farmers were entitled to buy 100 sheep for 127 pounds. With money that Oumam had hidden they were able to buy six cows for 111 pounds and two chickens and a cock (for 4/6 each – four shillings and six-pence). Oudad then had to wait his turn to get a tent wagon with a span of mules for the trek back to De Bank in Bothaville, which took several days.

As soon as Oupa Preller was re-established at De Bank, Oudad Jan together with his family (Oumam Lizzie and baby Hennie) relocated to Rustpan, starting all over again on the 23rd February 1902.

Whilst writing this story, I was fascinated by the fact that there were 40 – yes, forty – prisoner of war camps world-wide, and with India being host country to no less that 17 POW camps. Oudad Jan had mentioned Umballa, Bhim Tal, Ahmednagar, Bellary, Murree Hills, Kakool and Upper Topa. This led to further research to list all the camps and specifically to find our more of the various Geldenhuys' who died during the war. Oudad Jan was but one of the 27 000 Boers that was taken prisoner – and 24 000 that were shipped overseas.

The 40 POW/ Concentration Camps

Painting of Boer families burying their dead outside a British concentration camp in South Africa.

Farm burnings and burying loved ones

Concentration Camps

'Concentration camps' were established in South Africa to accommodate Boer families displaced as a result of Britain's scorched earth policies. The camps were poorly conceived and ill equipped to deal with the large numbers of detainees.

While the clearance and destruction of farms by British forces (including New Zealand troops) was intended to remove the main source of support for the Boer commandos, the real victims were the women and children who were left to fend for themselves. Aware that these families lacked shelter, food or protection from African marauders, the British hurriedly constructed camps to house them.

At least 40 concentration camps were constructed, altogether holding some 150,000 Boer refugees. Some, such as Merebank, which housed over 9000 internees, were so large that they resembled small towns. Sixty camps were also constructed to house the 115,000 native Africans who had worked as servants for the Boers.

Due to their hasty conception and the difficulties of accommodating a displaced population, the camps offered the bare minimum in terms of housing and supplies; many internees were forced to live in tents. Overcrowding and unsanitary conditions led to disease outbreaks, with typhoid, malaria, measles and dysentery being rife. Many British doctors and colonial nurses were shocked by the traditional remedies often employed by the Boers: one supposed cure for typhoid involved placing the warm stomach of a freshly slaughtered sheep on the patient's chest.

The use of concentration camps drew heavy criticism. Sir Henry Campbell-Bannerman, the leader of the Liberal Party in Great Britain, declared the camps to be 'methods of barbarism'. Others, such as social reformer Emily Hobhouse, inspected the camps (much to the ire of the military) and publicised the terrible conditions. As a result of pressure from the public, the British authorities began to improve conditions in the camps.

Towards the end of 1901 these criticisms, combined with a desire to end the war, caused the British to adopt a new policy regarding displaced Boer families. Rather than being removed to camps they were instead to be left to fend for themselves.

This tactic was aimed at burdening the Boer commandos so that they would be unable to continue their guerrilla warfare.

The suffering experienced in the camps left a lasting legacy of bitterness amongst the Boers. As a result of the poor conditions the mortality rate was high. Up to 28,000 Boers died, with 80% of the deaths being among children. Although the British did not keep records of the death toll among native Africans in the camps, it is believed that up to 15,000 died.

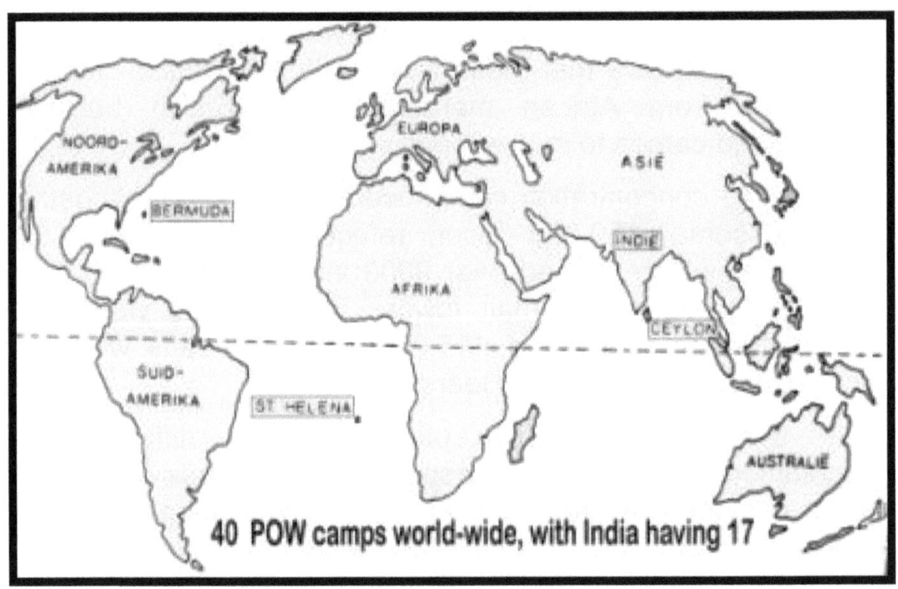

40 POW camps world-wide, with India having 17

The camps, with brief notes, were located as follows:

South Africa

Bellevue – Simonstown
Groenpunt / Green Point – Cape Town
Tin Town – Ladysmith
Umbilo – Durban

Bermuda – approx 4620

Burts Island – punishment camp and mainly Cape rebels.
Darrell Island
Hawkins Island – punishment camp and Cape rebels.
Hinson Island – children (like 7-year old Johannes van Heerden)
Long Island - cemetery
Morgans Island

Ports Island – hospital camp
Tuckers Island – pro-British camp

Ceylon – approx 5125

Diyatalawa
Hambantota
Mount Lavinia – recuperation
Ragama – punishment / hard labour
Urugasmanhandiya – pro-British camp

India – more than 9000

Abbottabad
Ahmednagar
Amritsar (Fort Govindgarh – punishment camp)
Bellary
Bhim Tal
Dagshai – parole camp
Kaity-Nilgiris
Kakool
Murree Hills
Satara – parole camp
Shahjahanpur
Sialkot
Salon
Trichinopoly
Umballa
Upper Topa
Wellington

St Helena – approx 5000

Broadbottom
Deadwood No 1
Deadwood No 2 – pro-British camp
Fort High Knoll – punishment camp
Jamestown – parole camp
RAMC – hospital

Portugal

Abrantes
Alcobaca

Caldas da Rainha
Fort Peniche
Fort de São Juliao da Barra
Tomar

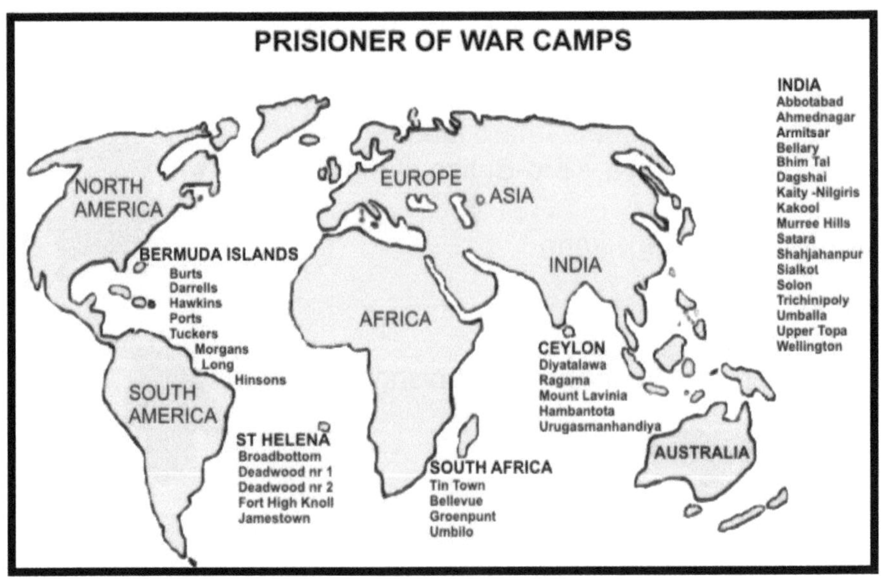

The youngest Boer child prisoner of war to die was eight-year old David Mathys Jacobs who died of measles at Bellary. The eldest fatalities were 74-year old Barend Johannes Liebenberg and Arnoldus Mauritz Meiring who died in St Helena.

Geldenhuis / Geldenhuys casualties are listed in the Roll of Honour.

Jan Geldenhuys' Anglo-Boer War diaries provides a very valuable first-hand account of my grandfather's experience as an early coloniser in Africa but who resisted the British onslaught against the Afrikaner (a Boer). Having read most books about the Anglo-Boer War, I found very little about life in the POW camps in India, and also very little mention of Abram Preller and Ernst van Biljon. The odd 'Geldenhuys' has been mentioned, serving under General Beyers, in the Waterberg area – north of Pretoria (Old Nylstroom / Warmbaths region). Oumam Lizzie mentioned that Oudad Jan had deployed there after the fall in enemy hands of Bloemfontein and Pretoria (both Boer republic capital cities). However, to return to Ernst van Biljon - - nowhere else did I find out that Ernst lost both his wife Kitty and two children in the Klerksdorp concentration camp – and this must have broken his spirit resulting in the frequent hospital trips he made at Umballa. Readers may recall that Oudad Jan went to the hospital on the eve of his departure, to bid farewell to his very good room-mate. Oudad did not show or describe much emotion regarding the parting. It must have been demoralising if not devastating!? Oudad Jan did not dwell on his own feelings even when he lost his own child when Oumam Lizzie was interned in the Kroonstad Concentration camp. This knowledge prompted Rina and I to do a detour to the Orange River Concentration Camp, where the present owners of the Doornbult farm, Rina Wiid, gave us a personalised conducted tour of this very well preserved Battlefields route tourist attraction.

Oumam lived in Bothaville until her death on 5th April 1976. She was buried next to my grandfather on Rustpan. The inscribtion on her headstone reads*"Hier rus moeder, tot die dag breek" - here Mother rests, till day break.*Her grave is next to Oudad Jan's.

Rustpan - Bothaville district

A visit to "Die Oranjerivierkampe" is highly recommended – as is a visit to Belmont, Magersfontein, Paardeberg and Kimberley and I trust that Lucy Geldenhuys will one day tread in the footsteps of her grandmother – Rina Geldenhuys.

New Zealanders and the Boer War

The South African War (Boer War) was the first overseas conflict to involve New Zealand troops. Fought between the British Empire and the Boer South African Republic (Transvaal) and its Orange Free State ally, it was the culmination of longstanding tensions in southern Africa.

Eager to display New Zealand's commitment to the British Empire, Premier Richard Seddon offered to send troops two weeks before conflict broke out. Hundreds of men applied to serve, and by the time war began in October 1899, the First Contingent was already preparing to depart for South Africa. Within a few months they would be fighting the Boers.

By the time peace was concluded two and a half years later, ten contingents of volunteers totalling over 6500 men (plus 8000 horses) had sailed for Africa, along with doctors, nurses, veterinary surgeons and a small number of school teachers. Seventy-one New Zealanders were killed in action or died of wounds, with another 159 dying in accidents or as result of disease.

The South African war set the pattern for New Zealand's later involvement in the two world wars. Specially raised units, consisting mainly of volunteers, were despatched overseas to serve with forces from elsewhere in the British Empire. The success enjoyed by these troops fostered the idea that New Zealanders were naturally good soldiers, who required minimum training to perform well.

Coromandel Combatants

New Zealand rallied to Britain's aid when the Anglo-Boer War started in 1899.

The first casualty came from the small Coromandel town of Paeroa in which I have made my home - since November 2013. That casualty is Bradford, whose commemoration plague is displayed on a prominent hill feature overlooking the town. I made it my business to visit the local museum and Returned Servicemen's Association (RSA) to learn more about this brave Kiwi who sacrificed his life 115 years ago.

THIS MEMORIAL
WAS ERECTED BY PUBLIC SUBSCRIPTION
IN MEMORY OF
GEORGE ROLAND BRADFORD
SERGT MAJOR 2ND BATTALION (HAURAKI)
INFANTRY VOLUNTEERS
DIED OF WOUNDS RECEIVED AT JASFONTEIN,
SOUTH AFRICA, 18TH DECEMBER 1899
HE WAS THE FIRST FROM ANY OF THE COLONIAL
CONTINGENTS TO GIVE HIS LIFE FOR THE EMPIRE
"A SOLDIER AND A MAN"

George Roland Bradford

George Bradford from Paeroa was the first colonial soldier to die in the Boer War. Richard Stowers

Significantly, it should be noted that George Bradford was the first combatant from any of the Colonial contingents to give his life for the Empire. He died of wounds received at Jasfontein on the 18th December 1899. He was serving as Sergeant Major of the 2nd Battalion (Hauraki) Infantry Volunteers.

Local historical records would suggest that his inferior horsemanship may have been the cause of his falling into Boer hands - and a probable lack of superior medical facilities may have resulted in an untimely death. Never the less, I hereby wish to record my deepest respect for him and his descendants for sacrificing his life, albeit for Queen and Country.

I will henceforth pay due respects at the annual ANZAC parades in remembrance of his bravery. Every time I venture up Primrose Hill I will make it my business to remember him.

George Roland Bradford - Primrose Hill, Paeroa, NZ

My visit to the Memorial prompted me to research other Kiwi personalities that made war against the opposing Boer forces - because of my own grandparent's involvement in the conflict. This interest meant that I started collecting Anglo-Boer War memorial photographs. Starting in the Coromandel, I found numerous monuments, in fine condition let me hasten to add, that adds a richness and different perspective to that inherited from my parents and grandparents. I trust my own grandchildren will cherish these endeavours. Perhaps not while

I am still alive, but at some future date when the dust may be dusted after rediscovering this booklet.

Maybe names like Walter Calloway, George Roland Bradford and Dick Hubbard will have some reverence for Geldenhuys in future. Primrose Hill is a fine starting point.

Ohinemuri Regional History Journal 12, October 1969

By C. W. Malcolm, B .A.

The No.1 Ohinemuri Rifles was formed on 16th June, 1897 at Paeroa. In 1898, together with the Te Aroha, Karangahake, Waihi, Coromandel, and Onehunga groups the Ohinemuri Rifles were incorporated into the Second Battalion Auckland Rifle Volunteers. The first Commanding Officer was Major Thomas Nepean Edward Kenny (late 73 Royal Highlanders and 23 Royal Welsh Fusiliers). A well-respected, soldierly figure in Paeroa, George Roland Bradford, formerly of the famous Coldstream Guards, was appointed Battalion Sergeant-major on 27th January, 1899. In that year the integrity of the British Empire was threatened by the growing antagonism of the Boers in South Africa. Anticipating war, volunteers enlisted to be ready if the worst happened.

In Paeroa the names of six men stood on the list: Avery, Bradford, Hubbard, McPherson, Shaw, and Tetley. War came! They assembled. McPherson was the farthest off, sleeping in his bunk at Waitekauri, where he was awakened by a messenger who had led a horse there for him to ride through the night, arriving in Paeroa with the dawn to join his waiting companions. By long train journey (in those days) to Auckland. By boat from Onehunga, and so to Wellington where the First Contingent was assembling with their horses for the sea voyage to Cape Town. The use of horses in war is, of course, a thing of the past, but not the least of the miseries of these noble beasts was the frightful sea-sickness that assailed them on their long journey to the Cape. They sailed on 21st October, Trafalgar Day,1899.

On 18th December, 1899, Bradford mounted horse to ride to battle at Jasfontein. I have heard my late uncle, Trooper William McPherson, and the late P. R. Hubbard say that, excellent soldier that he was, Bradford was no expert horseman. Hubbard it was who, on that fatal morning, assisted Bradford to the saddle and bade him good-bye and good luck.

Wounded in the battle, Bradford fell into the hands of the Boer's. Had he been a more skilled rider he might perhaps have made good his escape and received better medical attention in his own lines. Who can say? In captivity, he died of his wound and was buried by alien hands in an unmarked grave in a foreign land. He was the first from any of the Colonial Contingents to give his life for the Empire.

His monument, until recently wrecked by vandal hands, stood in tribute on Tuikairangi (Primrose Hill, Paeroa) for many years since its unveiling at the turn of the century by the Right Hon. Richard John Seddon, P.C., LL.D., the Prime Minister of New Zealand who has gone down in History as "King Dick". It bears the inscription: This fountain was erected by Public subscription in memory of George Roland Bradford Sgt. Major Second Battalion (Hauraki) Infantry Volunteers who died of wounds received at Jasfontein - South Africa, 18th December, 1899.

"A Soldier and a Man".

Since Mr. Malcolm wrote the above article and accompanying poem, the Bradford Memorial has been restored by the Paeroa Borough Council. The large top ornamental section had been smashed beyond repair so this was replaced by a specially selected stone, donated by Mr. C. Bradford, from the "White Rocks" Karangahake.

On Anzac Day this year when a Service was held at the adjacent Cenotaph a wreath was laid at 'the Bradford Memorial by Mr. Fred Hubbard M.C. whose late brother 'Dick' had also served during the Boer War. (Editor)

THE FOUNTAIN

C.W. Malcolm

The cenotaph in Whitehall stands
Where wreaths are placed by Royal hands
Midst mournful music of her bands
Remembering men in far-flung lands
Who heard the Empire call.
In London's heart the Abbey lies
And St. Paul's dome lifts to the skies
Its golden cross of sacrifice

Recalling men who paid the price
Who heard the Empire's call.
At sacred shrines we homage pay
To mighty Empire passed away !
At sunset of her glorious day
Honouring men of noble clay
Who heard the Empire call.
A forlorn fountain on a hill
Recalls us to our homage still –
To Bradford who, of his free will,
Answered the trumpet sounding shrill
That was the Empire's call.
Briton and Boer in War arrayed.
Across the veld in conflict swayed;
He rode to battle unafraid,
And fell in combat, undismayed –
For 'twas the Empire's call
And he the first to fall
In answer to her call

The Engagement at Jasfontein.

'New Zealanders in Action' was a graphic account of the engagement at Jasfontein, in which fight the New Zealanders took part, is from the N.Z. Herald's reporter with General French's force:-

ARUNDEL Military Camp, Dec 23 1899

After the reorganisation of the forces upon the arrival of General French, the commanding officer had drawn up a plan of campaign for the following day, Monday 19.

At a quarter to three a.m. on the date mentioned, while the New Zealanders were enjoying well-earned rest, after their arduous labours of the previous week, they were aroused from their slumbers by the guard. "Up there, you men," was the order passed rapidly from tent to tent, and the Maorilanders, surprised, jumped up hastily to obey the command. No questioned were asked, but with soldier-like rapidity, the men quickly obeyed the word of command. Tunics were donned, boots fastened, bandolier, belt, and water bottles, were quickly swung, leggings and spurs fixed, horses uncovered and saddled, and in eight minutes from the word of command the New Zealanders were in their saddles and ready for action. Each man had 50 rounds of ammunition for his Martini-Enfield, 50 in his bandolier, and 100 in his pouch.

Dawn was just breaking as the men drew up, and soon the subdued light of the rising sun shone over the dark coloured bush-dotted height of Artillery Hill, heralding the advent of the orb of day, whose piercing rays beat daily down upon those on the veldt, where subsequently the heat waves radiate, scorching faces and smarting eyes, and creating a thirst that even frequent recourse to the water-bottle cannot quench. As the golden rays grew brighter and brighter and the rock-covered peaks of the hills to the east stood out more distinctly against the lightening sky beyond, the Royal Horse Artillery rumbled slowly up, and the headquarters' staff, General French and staff officers, appeared. It was then recognised that some important movement was contemplated, known only to the headquarters' staff and officers (Major Robin being in command of the No's 1 and 2 of the New Zealand contingent, with Captains Davis and Maddocks in immediate charge of the North and South Island companies). The destination of the companies was Jasfontein, lying about south of the Boers' main position, and distant from the camp about eight miles.

The object of the exhibition was a reconnaissance in force to ascertain the strength of the enemy. As the sun rose higher and higher, its rays were cast over kopjes, bergs, and veldt, the forces moved from the camp, passing through the neck between Artillery Hill and the range intervening, turned in an easterly direction, and crossed the veldt between Sandadam and the kopjes skirting the (NZ) camp. No sign of the enemy could be seen, and beyond the tread of the New Zealand horses - muffled considerably by contact with the dust, and the rumble of the artillery gun carriages - no sound could be heard. Far off, the heights beyond Jasfontein, our destination, glittered and shimmered in the morning sun, now rising proudly above the range of hills. Below, in the valley, between the Boers' stronghold and the kopjes, from which the enemy had been shelled on previous occasion, and in which engagement the New Zealand took a prominent part, the clumps of trees hide the farm from view.

As we draw nearer and nearer to the guns of the Boers, the chatter of the men ceased, countenances grew sad, and a firm, determined look unconsciously spread over the faces of the New Zealanders and the Royal Horse Artillery. Close attention was paid to rifles; bandoliers were examined, and girths and saddles tested. We halted about 3000 yards distant from the farm. Orders were smartly given and promptly obeyed.

The guns were unlimbered, and bang! Boom! The 12-pounders were merrily pounding away shell after shell; shell was poured into the vicinity of the farm where there was any cover likely to afford hiding places for the Boers existed. As the men remembered the hot fire that had played from this quarter on a previous occasion and thought of fallen comrades, they set to work determined to wipe out old scores. The guns were splendidly trained, and the artillery did good work. The General, who watched the result of the shelling with considerable interest, gave the order to cease firing, and thus the New Zealanders knew their turn had come.

The expectant, almost pleased look, on their faces showed that they were eager for the fray, and that with them it was a case of fighting to the finish, if such a course met with the approval of the General. Remembering that the Jasfontein farm had been well occupied by the Boers on the occasion of the previous engagement, both officers and men expected a warm encounter when the farm was reached, but I question whether any men present anticipated that one of the hottest engagements of the campaign was to ensue.

No 1 Company, under Captain Davis, were first ordered to advance, and scarcely had the words of command been uttered when the New Zealanders, in their picturesque uniform and with hats stuck jauntily on one side, moved forward with alacrity nearer and nearer to the farm, and yet no sign of the enemy. But the men are now becoming familiar with the peculiar fighting tactics adopted by the Boers, and every man was on the qui vive. At last the farm was reached, and a party ordered to search the house and surroundings, while a close watch was kept on the clumps of trees and boulders on the adjoining kopjes in case of a surprise. The farm was thoroughly searched, and nothing of importance discovered. The beds had been slept in the previous night, but the occupants had probably fled to the ranges when firing commenced. After a thorough search of the house and gardens, the party were ordered to retire and occupy another position.

Before this could be done, however, the Boers suddenly appeared galloping over the first kopje on the right, and taking up a position almost abreast of the party. To counteract this movement, which was evidently the first of a series, arranged to trap the New Zealanders and the artillery, and capture the guns, and probably also to capture the General and headquarters staff if they remained close enough to the main body, men were sent across to the right to intercept the Boer party. They galloped across the Karroo, and made straight for the Boers in a most plucky manner, but were stopped by a barbed wire fence. A movement on the kopje to the right, and the appearance of a number of Boers on the right showed the Boers had entrenched themselves in two good fighting places, and had a decided advantage in this respect. The danger of the position was at once recognised, and the men ordered to get under cover. The major portion of men managed to get close to the farmhouse, but the others had no time to retire when the Boers appeared on the right, and at a distance of about 800 yards opened fire on our men.

The New Zealanders responded most pluckily, and their aim being better than that of the enemy many a Boer lost the number of his mess. The New Zealanders who were in the “tight corner” numbered about 70, and the Boers, it is estimated, were about 300 or 400 strong. The odds, therefore, were decidedly in favour of the enemy. For twenty minutes a hot fire was kept up, but the Boers were bad marksmen, and their shots went wide. As the New Zealanders sought cover, the Boers evidently made a supreme effort to cut them off from the main body. A perfect hailstorm of bullets was rained on them, and the party were enveloped in dust from the bullets striking sun-dried Karroo. Away to the north the big guns from the Boers were booming away, the shells hurtling over the plain, and sending up large clouds of dust that at times almost enveloped the party on the Karroo. But the little party fought on, seeking shelter at time, and surrounded by a cloud of dust as the bullets rattled on the plain. The men appeared to bear charmed lives, and with many a shout of encouragement fought bravely and well. They were steady as rocks, and obeyed the word of command as though on parade.

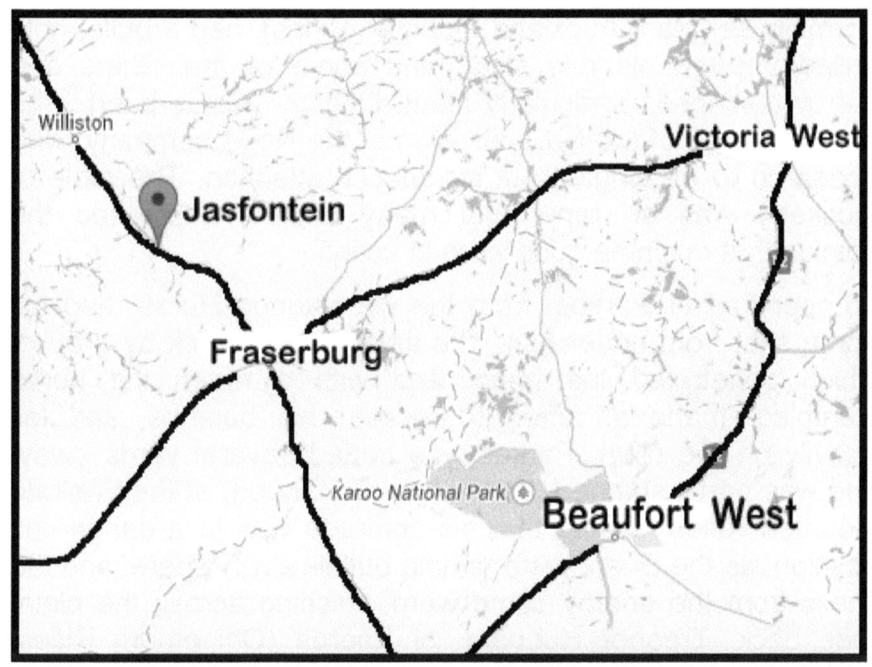

Map of Jasfontein situated Eastern Cape

In the nullah to the right of a wire fence, the same fence that had prevented the New Zealanders from cutting off the first party of Boers that appeared on the kopje to the right, Trooper Bradford, of Paeroa, Auckland, a member of the Ohinemuri Rifles, was heading for the farmhouse for shelter when he was shot in the leg somewhere between the knee and the hip. Those that saw him fall say that he was riding towards the farmhouse, when suddenly groaned, placed his hand on his groin, crying, “I've got one!” pitched over the horse's shoulder on the ground, striking his head as he fell. The blood welled from his wound, turning the light brown of the Karroo to a darker colour. Some of the New Zealanders attempted to get near their wounded comrade, with the intention of taking him back, but such a fulisade of bullets was rained upon them that they could not stand up against it. Bradford lay as though dead. He was resting on his side, with his head lying on a small flat stone, his knees drawn up and his head twisted round. He was believed to be dead, and in fact was reported as such.

Several of our men had most miraculous escapes, Thus, Trooper Maunder, Waikato Mounted Rifles, had his water bottle pierced through the neck, and was wounded in the wrist. Trooper Tubman, Canterbury Mounted Rifles, had a bullet hole drilled through his wallet and overcoat. Trooper Casey (formally sergeant Auckland Mounted Rifles), had a bullet hole drilled through his rifle sling, and some of the others had narrow escapes, particularly Lieut. Lindsay (Canterbury), who was in charge of the No. 2 division of the No. 1 company, who appeared to be singled out for special attention. The rattle of musketry was so rapid that many officers expressed the opinion that machine guns were in action.

Trooper Farrier Parkes, from the Heretaunga Horse, had his horse shot from under him. The animal was struck by a bullet which penetrated the head, and with a moan the horse stumbled, made an effort to recover his balance, and fell heavily on the plain. Parkes was hurled several yards away, and was partly stunned, but Sergeant Mahood, of the Waikato Mounted Rifles, seeing that his comrade was in a dangerous position, as the Boers were raining bullets everywhere, and the shells from the enemy camp were whistling across the plain, rode back. Trooper Hubbard, of Paeroa (Ohinemuri) Rifles, also noticed Parkes' plight, and despite the hail of bullets rode back and stood by him until he recovered his senses, and accompanied him to where Sergeant Mahood was waiting. Parkes mounted behind Mahood and the two New Zealanders returned to camp in this manner, amidst the cheers of those who witnessed the incident.

Several horses were wounded, but not seriously, and none of the riders were dislodged. The small party managed to get clear of the kopje, and secured shelter on the farm, when the Boers recommenced shelling operations, and pitched shell after shell dangerously near the spot where the little band of New Zealanders were clustered. The General ordered Major Robin to retire the whole force, and this was done in splendid style. The companies of New Zealanders became united, the retirement from the farm being made in an interval between volleys from the enemy. The Mounted Infantry then joined the artillery, which had been firing at the Boer camp, but although the Boers "Long Tom" could reach us (though it was just in range, about three miles), our 12-pounders were short, and it did not do much damage to the enemy's stronghold.

A return march was made across the veldt, and the party returned to camp about midday, after one of the hardest skirmishes of the campaign. The reconnaissance was distinctly successful, the enemy's exact position and strength being determined, as from where the forces were congregated a good view of the laager was obtained. The prominent part taken by the New Zealanders, the success that attended their operations drew forth unstinted praise from the General and members of the headquarters staff and officers of the Royal Horse Artillery. The scouting was excellent, the shooting well-timed and effective, and the general behaviour and discipline of our men a credit to themselves and to the colony from which they came.

The article was extracted and reproduced from the Poverty Bay Herald.

Percy Richard Hubbard

Hubbard was a Boer War veteran that has already been mentioned in despatches above.

He was born in Canterbury in 1876. Dick Hubbard as he was affectionately known to a host of friends went to school at Mangere and later helped his father on a farm there. In 1890 Mr Hubbard Senior, a pioneer family, purchased a large block of partly improved land at Komata near Paeroa and the whole family settled there, the property being carried on by Hubbard Brothers after the father's death in 1897.

He was a member of the Paeroa Company of Rifle Volunteers and on the call for troops for South Africa in 1899 he, along with five others, became members of the First Contingent, New Zealand Mounted Rifles. He took part in the Jasfontein battle, the relief of Kimberley and Mafeking. His comrades from Paeroa were Avery, G.R. Bradford, McPhereson, Shaw and Tetley. All but Bradford returned.

Dick Hubbard lived a full and fruitful life to be widely respected throughout the Thames Valley. He died in Auckland on 1st April 1968, aged 92, and left the Komata / Paeroa district a better place for having lived in it.

L.M. Tarrant

Leonard Matthews Tarrant is honoured as a Boer War casualty from Coromandel. His Regimental number was 71, on the First Contingent that departed for South Africa on the ship Waimea on 21 October 1899. His occupation was a miner, and rank a

Private. His next of kin was in Motueka, where his name also appears on a memorial

Coromandel Memorial

Further searches revealed that Leonard M Tarrant was considered as originating from Motueka and Nelson district

Motueka Memorial

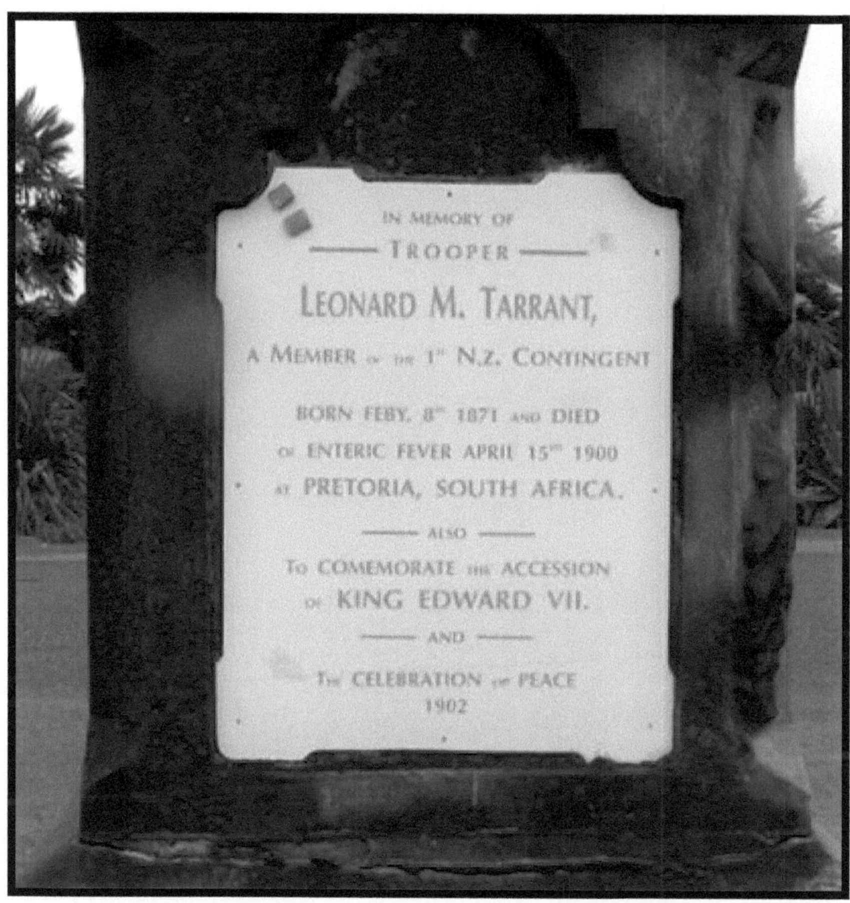

Leonard Tarrant, born 8 February 1871, died of enteric fever on the 15th April 1900 at Pretoria

Trooper Tarrant is also honoured on the Nelson Memorial

Nelson memorial

William Hardham VC

Wellington blacksmith William Hardham served in South Africa with the fourth New Zealand contingent. He was the only New Zealander to win the Victoria Cross in the South African War.

William Hardham Victoria Cross

The citation for his award, which appeared in the London *Gazette* on 4 October 1901, described his actions:

On the 28th January, 1901, near Naauwpoort, this non-commissioned officer was with a section which was extended and hotly engaged with a party of about twenty Boers.

Just before the force commenced to retire, Trooper McCrae was wounded and his horse killed. Farrier-Major Hardham at once went, under a heavy fire, to his assistance, dismounted, and placed him on his own horse, and ran alongside until he had guided him to a place of safety.

Bound to the 'Mother country' by the 'crimson tie' of empire, New Zealand sent more than 6500 volunteers and 8000 horses to South Africa. In all, 71 members of the 10 'contingents' were killed in action or died of wounds; 26 were accidentally killed, and 133 died of disease, more than half from typhoid fever.

Langverwacht Hill battle 23rd February 1902

On the 23rd February 1902, at Langverwacht Hill, south of Vrede, a Boer force broke through a British cordon at a point on the line held by New Zealand's Seventh Contingent. The New Zealand line consisted of small posts of five or six men in shallow trenches (sangars) along a ridge. During the night a small group of Boers drove a herd of cattle against the wire entanglements connecting the British blockhouses and used this distraction to overwhelm one of the New Zealand posts. They then advanced up the hill, attacking and destroying a number of other New Zealand-held posts. After ferocious close-quarter fighting, the Boers opened a gap through which most of their force escaped. The New Zealand casualties were high: of about 80 to 90 men in the front line, 23 were killed and more than 40 wounded. This was the first time that New Zealand forces suffered such heavy loss of life in an overseas conflict.

The 1 March 1902 issue of Christchurch's *Star* newspaper, under the heading of 'The Gallant Seventh', acknowledged 'a feeling of general sadness'. But it went on to add that 'we can't make cakes without breaking eggs. After all, the same number might soon have filtered away, one by one, the victims of enteric [typhoid fever]. These have at least had a chance to leave a glorious name, and they have done it'.

Photos - NZ History

Despite the setback at Langverwacht, the New Zealanders 'displayed great gallantry and resolution'. Throughout the war the New Zealand contingents were highly regarded. The *Times history of the war in South Africa* judged that once they had gained some experience, the New Zealanders were 'on average the best mounted troops in South Africa'.

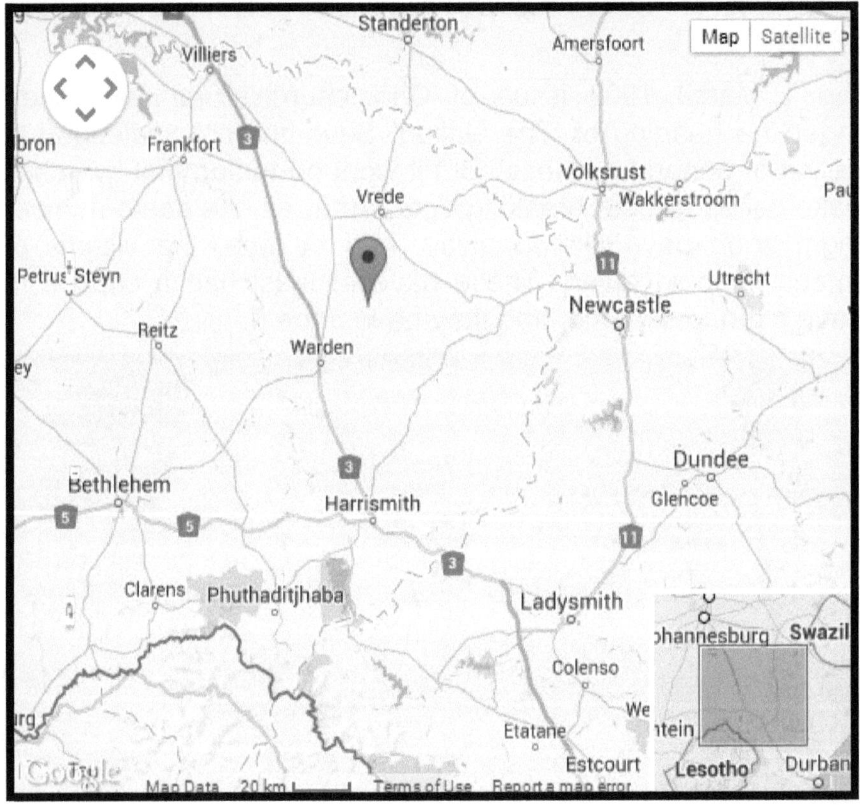

Battle of Langverwacht Hill 23 February 1902

In 1905 a memorial was erected on Langverwacht Hill to commemorate the New Zealanders who died. To represent the strength, constancy and long life of the British Empire, three oaks were also planted around the memorial. In late 2000 the memorial cairn was destroyed when an already weakened oak was toppled during a storm.

Walter Callaway

Walter Callaway

John Walter Callaway (Wāta te Wahahuia) is credited with being the first Māori to serve in the South African War. Walter, as he was commonly known, was born in 1873 in Kikawhakerere to a Cornish father, John Callaway, and a Māori mother, Huihana Te Arawaere, of Te Ngare hapū of Ngāi Te Rangi iwi. Being Māori, he defied the British dictum of the day that "no natives could fight in a white man's war.'

Raised in the Coromandel, Callaway was working as a miner when the outbreak of the war was announced. Already a member of the Coromandel Volunteer Rifles, he was selected, with three others, to join the remaining volunteers from the Auckland military district.

After arriving in South Africa with the First Contingent, Callaway served as both a despatch rider and as a scout, being recognised for 'Meritorious Service' by the British Commander-in-Chief, Field Marshal Lord Roberts. He served with the British forces that relieved the besieged town of Kimberley on 15 February 1900 and with those that managed to break the Boer defences at Driefontein, for which he was awarded the Driefontein clasp. During the remainder of his time in South Africa he took part in the advances into the Orange Free State and the Transvaal. Before departing for home on 3 November 1900 he was promoted to Lance Corporal.

Back in New Zealand, Callaway applied to return to South Africa and was assigned to the Seventh Contingent as Regimental Sergeant-Major. The Seventh took part in the treks that were aimed at countering the Boer commandos. On 22 July 1901 Callaway was wounded at the Battle of Witkop while risking his own safety to rescue two fellow soldiers. While galloping to the rescue of an Australian in dire danger, he was shot and almost fatally injured. As a result of his injury he developed malaria; although he recovered he returned home in December 1901.

Wishing to advance his career, Callaway applied once again to serve as an officer in South Africa. Although his application was rejected, he left for South Africa unofficially, hoping to rejoin the Seventh Contingent. Finding the Seventh was due to return to New Zealand, he transferred to the Ninth Contingent. He served with the Ninth during the peacekeeping process and was promoted to the rank of Lieutenant – making him one of the first Māori to become an officer in the NZ Army.

On his final return to New Zealand Calloway contracted smallpox, becoming the first recognised case of the disease in New Zealand. Although he managed to recover, his wounds and the effects of the illness left him weakened throughout the rest of his life.

Callaway's biography is the first published account of a Māori in the South African War (1899-1902) and also includes a supportive foreword by New Zealand's Chief of the Defence Force, Lieutenant General Mateparae. This true story reveals a forgotten hero in what many term as 'New Zealand's Forgotten War.' It tells not only about a remarkable soldier, but also highlights the horrors and hardships of a war, which a later

British Prime Minister described as 'infamous, criminal and wholly indefensible.'

He died on 16 September 1926.

By Simon Daisley

Boer War Memorials

War memorials hold a fascination for me. What started as Rhodesian War Memorials has now expanded to include the Boer war memorials - in South Africa and particularly the Coromandel region of New Zealand.

South African

Field Gun - Old Fort in Durban

Gideon Scheepers - shot by firing squad

Memorial in Albert Park, Durban

Banneling memorial - Bloemfontein

Black Watch - Magersfontein

Highland Brigade - Magersfontein

Kimberley Rhodes Memorial

Paardeberg - where General Cronje surrendered

New Zealand

New Zealanders put up about 50 war memorials to those who died in the South African war, most of which are still known to exist. All but one was completed within six years of peace. The memorials preserve in stone the imperial sentiments which inspired New Zealand's involvement in the war.

71 New Zealanders were killed in action and a further 133 died of sickness and 26 as a result of accidents. 6500 soldiers and 35 nurses were sent to South Africa during the course of 3 years of the war.

Over 50 Locations of NZ Boer War Memorials

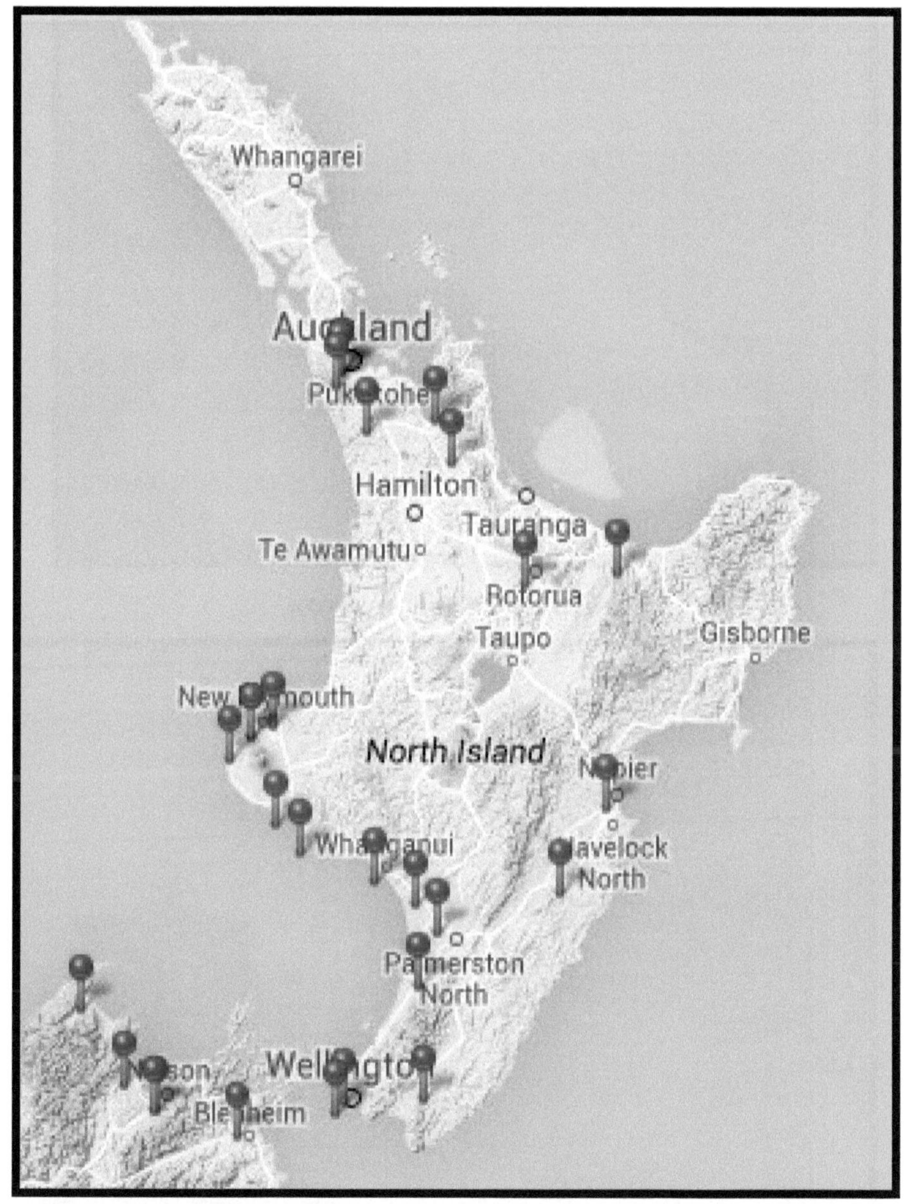

North Island locations

My particular interest is the Coromandel, and current home town of Paeroa.

Primrose Hill, Paeroa

Victoria Park, Thames

Thames - with names

IN HONOUR OF THOSE
WHO SERVED
IN MEMORY OF THOSE
WHO FELL
NEW ZEALAND WARS
BOER WAR

Hobsonville RSA - Auckland

Coromandel Town Memorial

Anglo-Boer War Roll of Honour

Lest we Forget

J. N. Geldenhuys, Wolmaranstad Commando, killed at Paardeberg, February 1900.

Jacobus Viljoen Geldenhuis, aged 46, died Diyatalawa camp 5th January 1901.

Maria Magdalena Preller, aged one and four months, died Kroonstad concentration camp, 5th April 1901.

Hettie Levina Geldenhuys, aged three and a half months, died Kroonstad concentration camp 15 August 1901.

Pieter Jacobus Geldenhuis aged 64, on board the Montrose troopship en-route to Bermuda, on 2nd September 1901.

Lourens Pieter A Geldenhuys, aged 68, died 22nd January 1902 and buried in the Kanatta cemetery, Colombo, Ceylon.

Jacobus Francois Geldenhuijs executed as a Cape Rebel at Graaff-Reinet on 14 February 1902.

Dorothea M Geldenhuys, aged 4, died Oranje River concentration camp, 15th February 1902

Hendrik P Geldenhuys, aged 62, died 21st May 1904 and buried in the Batticaloa cemetery in Colombo, Ceylon.

And all the 26 370 Afrikaner women and children breeding stock that died

Plus 4000 Boer combatants killed in action during the Three-Year War

The 71 New Zealand casualties, plus 159 dying in accidents or as result of disease.

And special mention of Paeroa casualty George Roland Bradford, died of wounds received at Jasfontein on the 18th December 1899.

At the going down of the sun, and in the morning,
We will Remember them.

Boer War Diaries of Geldenhuys

Our detour into Matjiesfontein was well worth the time – a place my grandmother Lizzie Preller spoke often about. She said that grandfather Jannie Geldenhuys and she would take a break en route to Cape Town to reflect on the Anglo-Boer War where the British had erected a monument to General Andy Waucup – who was killed in action during the battle of

Magersfontein (the British did not distinguish Magersfontein in the Northern Cape with Matjiesfontein in the Southern Cape.

During the War, a vast Remount Camp, with 10,000 troops and 20,000 horses, was established on the village outskirts. The veld southwest of the station is still littered with camp remnants including rusty old bully beef and biscuit tins. Part of the recently finished Hotel Milner served as a convalescent hospital for British officers and its central turret serving as armed look-out post. Matjiesfontein was also the site of the Old Courthouse where the trial of Boer hero Gideon Scheepers was held. Readers may recall my earlier report of how and why Scheepers was shot by the British as a Cape rebel – and the burning down of my grandmother's homes in Bothaville, because she had fed his commando when he passed briefly by their De Bank / Katbos View homes.

This bit of unfinished business convinced me to once again route via Graaff Reinet – to see whether I could find any untold history of the Scheepers assassination by the British.

We intentionally detoured via Graaff-Reinet to view the Scheepers display corner in the Military Museum section. We also looked at the Ivory serviette rings that Jan Petrus Geldenhuys brought back from the Ceylon prisoner–of-war camp. We concluded that it was his son – Jacobus Francois Geldenhuys who was executed by Firing Squad on that fateful St Valentines day in 1902 – 14th February - - with his name appearing immediately after that of G.J. Scheepers – Gideon. The charge sheets also attracted my attention.

Gideon was tried on the 18th December 1901 and shot a month later on the 18th January 1902. The day Gideon was shot is the same day that Jacobus Francois Geldenhuys was tried - - and he was shot on the 14th February 1902.

Geldenhuys's charges were for being active while armed, attempted murder and plundering. Scheepers' charges were 7 counts of murder, attempted murder, cruel behaviour, mistreating of prisoners, three counts of corporal punishment, destroying the railway line, destroying trains and sixteen charges of arson.

Gideon Scheepers look-a-like corner

Oudad Jan Geldenhuys, with his two sons Hendrik and Preller

INDEX

www.ingramcontent.com/pod-product-compliance
Ingram Content Group UK Ltd.
Pitfield, Milton Keynes, MK11 3LW, UK
UKHW041945190726
13854UKWH00004B/1793